Encyclopedia of

Marion Nichols

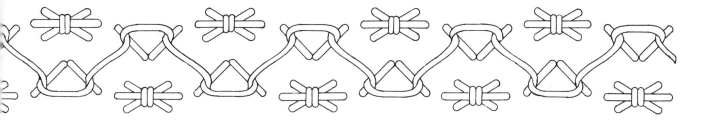

Embroidery Stitches, Including Crewel

Dover Publications, Inc., New York

Published in Canada by General Publishing Company,
Ltd., 30 Lesmill Road, Don Mills, Toronto, Ontario.
Published in the United Kingdom by Constable and Com-
pany, Ltd., 10 Orange Street, London WC 2.

Encyclopedia of Embroidery Stitches, Including Crewel is
a new work, first published by Dover Publications, Inc. in
1974.

International Standard Book Number: 0-486-22929-7
Library of Congress Catalog Card Number: 72-97816

Manufactured in the United States of America
Dover Publications, Inc.
180 Varick Street
New York, N.Y. 10014

To every little girl

who has cried over her stitches

I dedicate this book

Introduction

Embroidery stitches have long been used to enhance the beauty of fabric. Some stitches had a practical purpose in addition to being decorative. Much has been written on the subject of embroidery, and each writer has put forth a method to produce the desired effect. Having explored many of these methods, and being fundamentally lazy, I have decided that the best way is the easiest way for the individual to accomplish his or her purpose. Embroidery, as any hobby, should be fun. When we have to struggle for too long at any learning situation we become bored and go on to something else.

Like most little girls of my generation, I was required to do a bit of "fancy work" every day, and each stitch was laboriously taught to me. It was worked, ripped out and reworked, and many tears were shed until the required perfection was accomplished. Why, then, I ever picked up the embroidery needle again after I reached the age of reason, I shall never know. I truly believe that the reason few modern adults are passing this skill down to their daughters is that they too were exposed to embroidery in exactly the same manner. For a time the art of embroidery was rapidly becoming extinct in this country.

Then came a rebirth. Women found a need, in this pre-packaged, pre-frozen, pre-measured-mix age of ours, to express themselves creatively. With the help of modern printing methods, fabrics and yarns, and magazine exposure, embroidery became an available and exciting mode of self-expression. "I did it myself," became the happiest expression of the day. As more and more people found the joy of stitchery, the demand for more supplies and knowledge grew. Suddenly, everyone is doing it—or wants to try!

Why then write another book on stitchery? To sum up the complaints of my students, the problems seem to be these: "I'd love to do it but I don't know how"; "I know the stitch I want to use but I don't know the name of it"; "My needle never seems to be in the same position that the illustration shows"; "I can't hold my work in that position" and so forth.

The solution, then, seems to be a workbook that is specific enough to teach method to the novice and that can also serve the experienced as a reference.

These are the purposes of my book:

1. To arrange stitches in a logical order.

2. To identify embroidery stitches by their most logical and commonly used names.

3. To illustrate each stitch and step clearly, to avoid confusion. (As a further aid, the back of each stitch, shown in gray, is also illustrated. The back of a stitch is always represented as the mirror image of the stitch itself.)

4. To describe each step in sequence.

5. To suggest appropriate applications for the various stitches.

6. To relate easy stitches to more difficult ones, so that the learning process becomes a progressive expansion of skills.

7. To increase the "vocabulary" of stitches to the point where self-expression becomes a pleasure.

8. To encourage one's personal development of method.

I notice that as I work a step repeatedly, a rhythm develops, and I say a little phrase over and over to help me remember each step. It's just like dancing with your needle and thread! Wherever possible, I have drawn this rhythm and written the phrase. I must stress, however, that although the pattern fits me, you will have to adjust it to your own use. In the beginning the stitches you form will be uneven and your mo-tions will be awkward. Keep at it; practice; form the stitches over and over until each movement is smooth. Pay attention to the length of each stitch, the direction in which you are working, the tension required to make the stitch compati-ble with the material, and the direction in which the pull comes to complete the stitch. It soon becomes automatic.

How To Use This Encyclopedia Workbook

Identification of Stitches. Stitches, like folk songs, have been handed down from generation to generation and, like some songs, have many variations in name and method. Of course, the name and way *you* were taught is the correct and only way! However, the "loop" stitch *you* learned and the loop stitch *I* learned may be two entirely different stitches. This had led to much confusion. Therefore, I have tried to identify each stitch by the name most commonly used, and have listed its other names as well. Each and every stitch name appears in the index at the end of this book.

There are ten basic groupings or "families," keyed A through J. Each family has its own basic motion.

A. Straight stitches: an even up and down motion.

B. Back stitches: an encircling motion.

C. Chain stitches: a looping motion.

D. Buttonhole or blanket stitches: a cornering loop motion.

E. Fly or feather stitches: a swinging motion.

F. Cross stitches: a crossing motion.

G. Knotted stitches: a wrapping motion.

H. Composite stitches: a combination of two different motions.

I. Couched or laid stitches: a holding-down motion.

J. Woven stitches: an in-and-out motion.

Progression While Learning. The stitches in each family grouping are explained in order of progressive difficulty. I strongly suggest that novices begin with the first stitch in the family and master it before going on to the next. The more complicated stitches are sophisticated var-iations on more elementary stitches, and can only be fully appreciated if one has been exposed to the basic material.

The stitches within families are classified as follows:

Isolated: one stitch usually standing alone; the basic stitch.

Line: the basic stitch in various line arrangements.

Angled: the basic stitch worked at an angle.

Stacked: the basic stitch stacked up in a pile.

Grouped: a patterned arrangement.

Combined: further decoration of the basic stitch or its variations.

Refresher for Experienced Needlewomen. Working a stitch once or twice and mastering it does not necessarily imply remembering it forever. The simplest stitches, which are used over and over, will come to mind readily. However, it is handy to know where to find something special when you are feeling creative. For this reason I give a reminder of the basic rhythm, the direction of work, a list of appropriate uses and other miscellaneous remarks for each stitch.

Sampler Chart. A diagram of stitch placement is included at the beginning of each chapter. The diagram is in the shape of the area the stitch will cover—sometimes the actual line or lines to be covered; sometimes parallel lines which serve as a guide and sometimes geometric or natural shapes such as circles, squares or leaves. The name of each stitch is printed on the diagram.

Tips for Embroiderers

To Begin. Select a comfortable place to work with good over-the-shoulder light. Gather your supplies. Fabric will be preferably medium-weight linen or cotton. If you plan to make a sampler for each family, you will need ten pieces, each about 12" by 15". The design is based on an area roughly 8" by 11" (including borders) and the extra material allows for moving the hoople while work is in progress.

If, on the other hand, you plan to learn only a few stitches, these could be arranged on a long, narrow strip of material, as samplers were originally done. Stitches from many families can be arranged in a design suitable for framing or for making into a pillow.

Hoople. A 6- or 7-inch round wooden hoople (hoop or embroidery frame) with a screw adjustment is satisfactory for most embroidery situations. Hooples come in all sizes and shapes, and you may want others for different occasions. Place the smaller (inside) ring under the fabric at the area where you will be working. Force the larger ring over the linen and tighten the adjustable screw until fabric is held drum-tight. Remove the hoople when you are not working on the fabric, so it will not crease.

Needles. Purchase embroidery or crewel needles—short, sharp needles with long, slender eyes. Sizes 3, 4 or 5 are suitable for two-ply crewel wool. Tapestry needles or darners, sizes 17, 18 or 19 should be used for doubled or tripled two-ply wools, as well as for knitting or worsted yarns.

Threading is easy if you learn to do it properly. Double one end of the yarn over the eye of the needle and hold between thumb and forefinger of your left hand as if you were pinching salt. Withdraw the needle and, without releasing pressure, roll back thumb and forefinger just enough to see the yarn and push the eye of the needle down on the yarn, using a sawing motion. When you release your thumb and forefinger, enough yarn

will protrude so that you can pull it through. To save time keep threaded needles in a cork.

Yarn. Collect scraps of knitting yarns of various weights. When learning, it is not advisable to use anything heavier than a four-ply worsted. The stitches indicated on the samplers in this book are meant to be done with two-ply crewel yarn. This may be purchased at yarn and needlework shops and comes in many shades. Persian yarn is three two-ply strands loosely bundled together. Separate these strands when working unless a heavy stitch is desired. Sport weight or fingering yarn is also available and satisfactory.

Organize your yarn on a piece of cardboard to keep it neat. Cut the yarn into 30-inch lengths and organize by color. Cut a slit at each end of the cardboard, then just slip the threads into the slit at the top, loosely stretch them across the length of the cardboard, and slip the other ends through the slit on the other end of the cardboard.

Scissors. You will need a pair of small, sharp embroidery (or needlepoint) scissors to snip threads. Do not use them for cutting paper or fabric. Get good quality scissors and respect them; keep them in a case when not in use.

Thimble. Your thimble should fit the middle finger of your sewing hand tightly enough to stay on without pinching. Do use it; it takes a little while to get used to, but is well worth the effort. After setting the needle in place, push it through the fabric with the thimble, while pulling the point out of the fabric with thumb and index finger.

To Embroider. Choose a stitch. Place hoople on a sampler. Choose appropriate yarn and thread through needle. Weave end into fabric or tie small knot in end. Bring thread up at A and pull through. Follow A to B, etc., through individual stitch. End off on back by weaving threads in or tying a clove hitch (see knotted stitches, G.19). Cut the thread about ½ inch from the knot.

To Finish. After embroidery is finished it must be pressed. If it is soiled, it should be washed (gently in cold-water soap if *all* the materials used are washable) or dry-cleaned.

To avoid flattening stitches when pressing, place a heavy pad on the ironing board. I use an old sheet folded many times. Place the dry em-broidery face-down on the pad, cover with a damp pressing cloth (I use an old pillow case wrung out in cold water) and press until dry. Touch up around edges on front surface with point of iron, being careful not to flatten stitches.

Finished pieces may be made into pillows, framed as pictures, lined and mounted in a long strip as a bell-pull sampler, or inserted into a notebook encased in transparent acetate sheet protectors. These 8½'' by 11'' plastic envelopes are available at your local stationery store.

Contents

Glossary and Explanation of Symbols

Direction of Work (D.O.W.)   Start at end of arrow and work in direction of point. In stitches where there is no indication the direction is unimportant.

DNPF   Do Not Pierce Fabric. Slide needle between fabric and existing stitch.

Jacobean   Early seventeenth-century embroidery design usually based on tree of life pattern—curving trunks and branches supporting large imaginative flowers in muted colors. Early crewel embroidery used only these designs and was always worked on linen with fine, loosely spun, two-ply wool yarn. Today the word "crewel" can refer to many different embroidery designs; the only specific requirement seems to be wide usage of many variations of the basic embroidery stitches.

Journeys   Some stitches, like cross stitch, are partially completed in one direction and then finished on the return "trip." In embroidery, these trips are called journeys.

Warp   The threads that run lengthwise in a fabric, crossed at right angles by the woof (or weft) threads, which are the horizontal fillers.

Working Thread   That section of the thread which is closest to the hole through which it has just been drawn.

(T)   Tack stitch. Thread comes up from one side of stitch and goes back down in the same hole from the other side.

/   Pull thread through.

family

STRAIGHT STITCHES

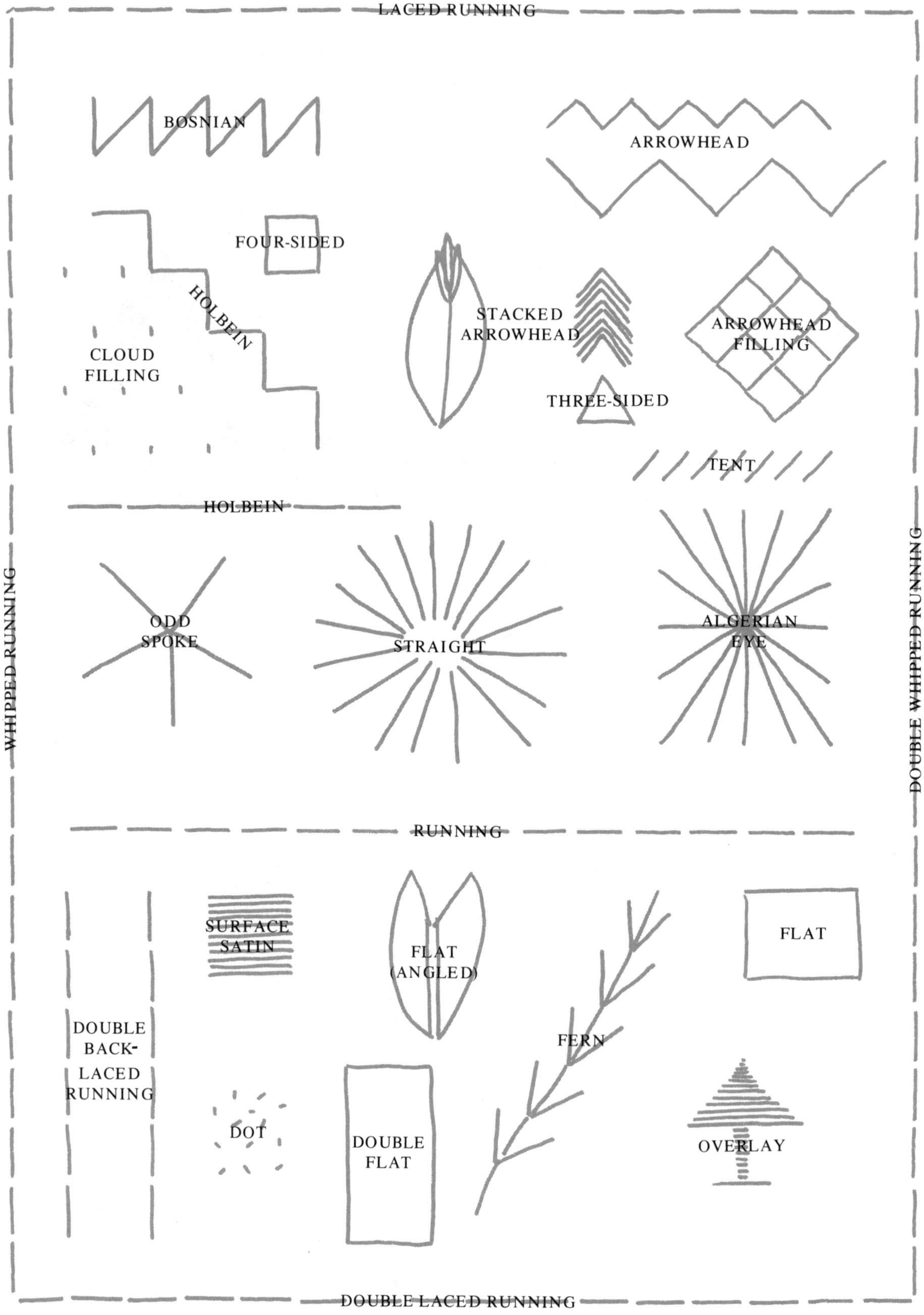
LACED RUNNING
BOSNIAN
ARROWHEAD
FOUR-SIDED
HOLBEIN
CLOUD FILLING
STACKED ARROWHEAD
ARROWHEAD FILLING
THREE-SIDED
TENT
HOLBEIN
WHIPPED RUNNING
DOUBLE WHIPPED RUNNING
ODD SPOKE
STRAIGHT
ALGERIAN EYE
RUNNING
SURFACE SATIN
FLAT (ANGLED)
FLAT
DOUBLE BACK-LACED RUNNING
FERN
DOT
DOUBLE FLAT
OVERLAY
DOUBLE LACED RUNNING

family A   Straight Stitches

Basic rhythm: simple up and down motion   →↑↓

Progression of difficulty

Isolated (Basic Stitch)   1. STRAIGHT (Stroke)

Variations   2. DOT (Single Seed, Seeding)

Line   3. RUNNING (Basting)
4. HOLBEIN (Double Running, Four-sided)

Angled   5. TENT (Half Cross)
6. ARROWHEAD AND FILLING (Three-sided)
7. BOSNIAN

Stacked   8. STACKED ARROWHEAD (Double Satin)
9. SURFACE SATIN (Stab Method)
10. OVERLAY (Patterned Running)
11. FLAT AND FILLING (Croatian Flat)
12. DOUBLE FLAT

Grouped   13. ODD SPOKE (Spoke, Wheel)
14. ALGERIAN EYE (Star Eyelet)
15. FERN

Combined   16. LACED RUNNING (Threaded Running)
17. WHIPPED RUNNING
18. DOUBLE BACK-LACED RUNNING
19. CLOUD FILLING

A.1 STRAIGHT STITCH
Stroke Stitch

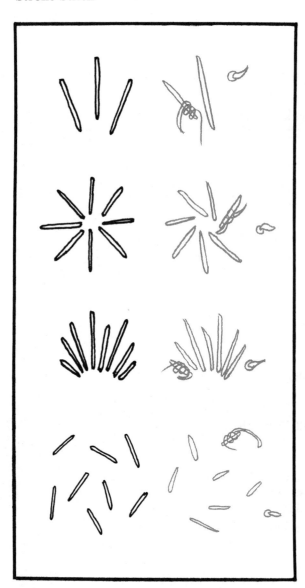

D.O.W. ←

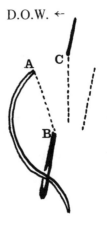

Step 1. Bring thread up at A; pull through. Insert needle at B, bring out at C; pull through.

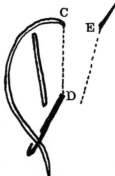

Step 2. Insert needle at D and bring out at E; pull through.

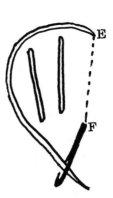

Step 3. Insert needle at F and pull through to back of work. Secure with clove hitch to finish. (See G. 19.)

RHYTHM
Up / over—down—up /

USES
Basis of many other stitches. Can be arranged in a circle to form a flower. Scattered hit or miss, but of uniform length, these stitches serve as a light powdery filling.

REMARKS
Draw a circle about the size of a quarter; mark center. With a dark gold thread, make many straight stitches coming almost to the center, like sunrays. With a lighter shade of gold, work over the same stitches again, and then a third time with a still lighter shade. This makes a lovely flower. Work center in French knots in a contrasting color.

RHYTHM
Up / over one space–down–up–change direction /
USES
Light powdery filling, Can be used to fill flower centers
or scattered lightly on a "hill" area in Jacobean designs.
REMARKS
Use darker colors; stitch will "get lost" if too light.

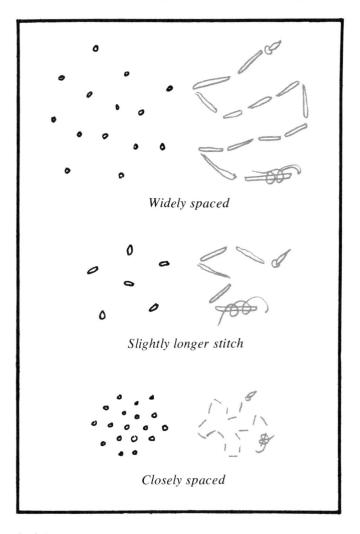

Widely spaced

Slightly longer stitch

Closely spaced

D.O.W. Any

Step 1. Bring thread up at A; pull
through. Insert needle at B (one fabric
thread away in any direction), bring
out at C; pull through.

Step 2. Insert needle at D at a different angle from A-B, bring out at C;
pull through.

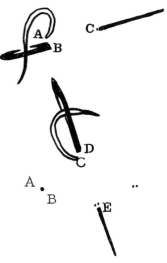

Note

Remember that each stitch should be
the same length and that each stitch
should slant in a different direction.
Spaces between stitches should be
uniform, but try to avoid a set pattern.

A.3 RUNNING STITCH
Basting

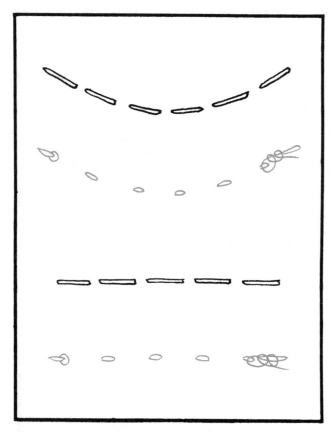

Step 1. Bring thread up at A; pull through. Insert needle at B, bring up at C; insert at D, bring up at E. Pull through.

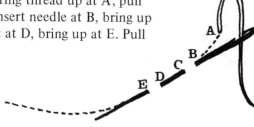

Step 2. Insert needle at F, bring out at G, etc. (If curve is gentle, several stitches may be picked up on the needle at one time. Work stitches one by one if curve is sharp.) Pull through.

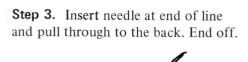

RHYTHM
Up / over–down–up /

USES
Thin line; follows a curve nicely. Can be used for outlining or as a foundation for many laced, whipped and woven decorative stitches.

REMARKS
Must be even: stitches uniform in length and spaces between stitches even. Keep stitch about three times as long as space between.

Step 3. Insert needle at end of line and pull through to the back. End off.

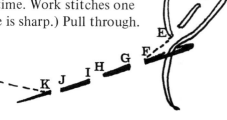

RHYTHM
Up / over–down / over–up /

USES
Borders, outlining, substitute for back stitch (saves on thread).

REMARKS
Proportion: equal distance between equal length of stitch; covers back and front alike and makes a neat back. Think "graphpaper" when working steps.

Called Holbein stitch because Hans Holbein portrayed it often in his paintings of the decorations on women's dresses. Basic stitch of "black-work," a type of embroidery.

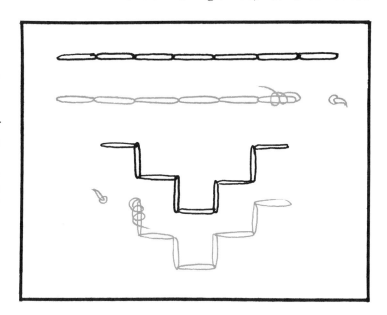

FIRST JOURNEY

Step 1. Bring needle up at A; pull through. Insert needle at B; pull through. Continue through H. (This "stabbing" up and down assures an even stitch, although stitch may be worked like regular running stitch.)

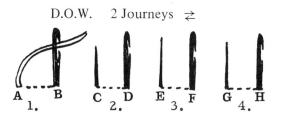

SECOND JOURNEY

Step 2. Bring needle up at G; pull through. Insert at F; pull through. Continue to end (B).

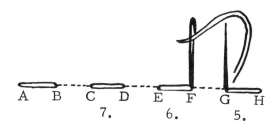

The figures at right show working method for another arrangement of Holbein stitch. Diagram shows second method of work but better accuracy is achieved using stab method. Four-sided stitch is formed when a second row is worked to complete the squares (I to H, G to F, etc.).

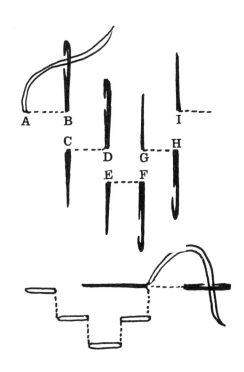

A.5 TENT STITCH
Half Cross Stitch

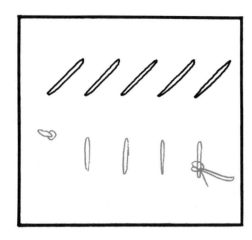

RHYTHM
Up / over–down–up /
USES
This stitch is common in needlepoint embroidery, where the yarn is wrapped around each thread of the canvas.
REMARKS
Must be worked evenly; picture graph-paper when working.
   Tent stitch is used for the first journey when making cross stitch (see F.1).

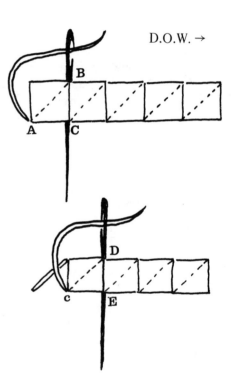

D.O.W. →

Step 1. Bring thread up at A and pull through. Insert needle at B and bring out at C; pull through.

Step 2. Insert needle at D and bring out at E; pull through.

Note

Squares, like graph paper, drawn in solid lines, are used to help place stitches evenly. Keep this in mind when working stitch.

RHYTHM
Up / down–angle–up /

USES
When "stacked" this makes an excellent filling stitch; try it on large leaf designs, Jacobean oval "flowers" etc., or in borders.

REMARKS
Think "graphpaper" on the diagonal when working, to keep stitches even.

Decorate with isolated stitches such as French knots, cross or star cross stitches in centers.

Arrowhead stitch is very attractive when laced with a second color. Try whipping (wrapping a constrasting color around each stitch).

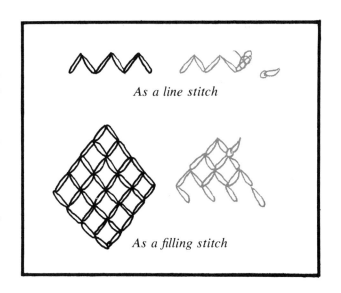

As a line stitch

As a filling stitch

D.O.W.   2 Journeys ⇄

FIRST JOURNEY

Step 1. Bring thread up at A; pull through.

Step 2. Insert at B, bring up at C; pull through.

Step 3. Repeat at D-E and F-G.

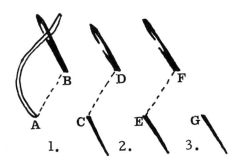

SECOND JOURNEY

Step 4. Insert needle at F, bring out at E; pull through. Repeat at D-C. Insert at B, pull through to back and knot to finish.

Three-sided stitch is made by completing each triangle. (A to C, C to E, E to G.)

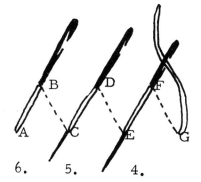

Note

When used as a filling stitch, all stitches in one direction should be worked first, and then all stitches in the other direction. This method tends to keep the work more even.

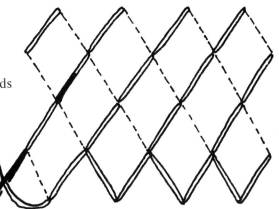

9

A.7 BOSNIAN STITCH

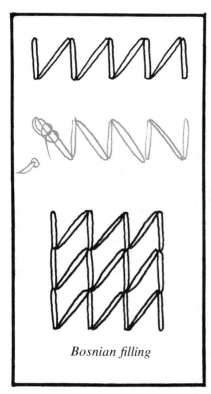

Bosnian filling

RHYTHM
Up / down–slant–up /

USES
Even borders, area filling.

REMARKS
Work evenly, thinking "graph paper."

The easiest way in which to make the filling stitch is to work all the perpendicular (alternate) stitches first, and then go back and work all the intervening diagonal stitches.

D.O.W. ⇆ 2 Journeys

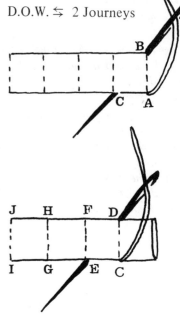

FIRST JOURNEY

Steps 1 and 2. Bring needle up at A; pull through. Insert needle at B, bring out at C; pull through. Insert needle at D, bring out at E; pull through. Continue until line is covered.

SECOND JOURNEY

Steps 3 and 4. Bring needle up at I; pull through. Insert needle at H and bring up at G; pull through. Insert at F, bring up at E; pull through. Continue until all diagonal stitches are made.

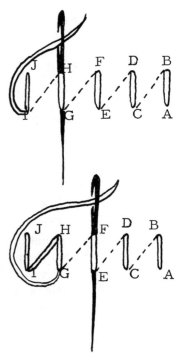

D.O.W. ↓

Step 1. Bring needle up at A; pull through. Insert at B, bring up at C; pull through.

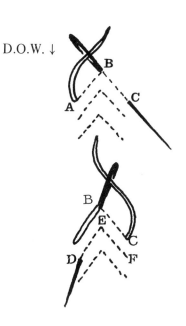

Step 2. Insert needle again at B, bring up at D; pull through. Continue until each arrowhead is completed. Do not work too closely to previous stitch.

TO FILL A LEAF-SHAPED AREA

Bring thread out at A; pull through. Insert needle at B, bring out at C; pull through. Keep stitches very close.

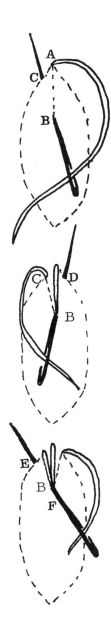

Insert needle again at B and bring out at D; pull through.

Insert needle again at B, bring out at E and pull through. (Three straight stitches in one hole at B give the leaf a pointed shape.) Complete leaf shape by making arrowheads, closely spaced, to bottom of area.

RHYTHM
Up / down–angle right down–up /

USES
Wide borders, arrowhead shapes, filling stitch for leaf shapes.

REMARKS
The leaf shape is easy to work if you always start just to the left of the first straight stitch (out and down a little each time), and remember that when the working thread is on the left, you start a new hold just below the first stitches. Then, when the thread is on the right, you go back into the same hole, so that each hole has two stitches branching out from the center.

A.9 SURFACE SATIN STITCH (Stab Method)

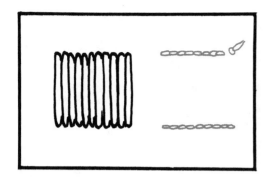

RHYTHM
Stab up / stab down

USES
Wide borders or lines.

REMARKS
Advantage: saves thread. Almost all thread is on top of fabric. If you had to raise your own sheep, shear, clean, card, spin, and dye your own wool, you'd use this stitch, too, as our pioneer grandmothers did!

Disadvantage: difficult to keep uniform. The twist of the yarn makes some threads fall out of line and makes work look uneven.

FIRST JOURNEY   D.O.W. ⇄ 2 Journeys

Step 1. Bring thread up at A; pull through. Insert needle at B (on lower line) and pull through.

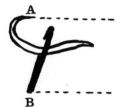

Step 2. (Needle is behind fabric.) Bring needle up at C on lower line (space between B and C is the width of one thread). Pull through. Insert needle at D on upper line; pull through, then bring up at E, keeping space between D and E the same as between B and C. Continue to end of area.

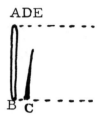

SECOND JOURNEY

Step 3. Bring thread up at M (lower line between last two stitches) and pull through.

Step 4. Insert needle at N (upper line between last two stitches) and pull through. Bring needle up on upper line between second and third stitch, and continue, filling spaces between stitches until area is covered. When finished, no fabric shows between stitches.

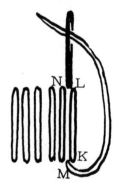

RHYTHM

Up / down–over–up / (More than one stitch may be picked up on the needle before pulling through, if desired.)

USES

A complete design in any geometric shape may be worked using only this stitch.

REMARKS

Any even-weave fabric such as corduroy or faille or one with a pronounced warp or weft will help keep this work even. It's fun to watch this one grow. Look at any primitive weaving (such as that from Guatemala) for inspiration.

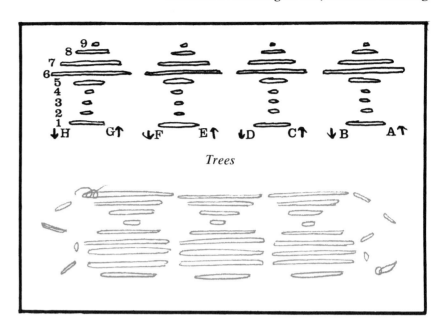

Trees

Work this stitch (as a regular running stitch from right to left) on an even-weave material, counting threads between stitches for best effect. It is easiest to work from the bottom of the design up (rows are numbered for order). Keep rows close together.

D.O.W. ↑

Note

Arrows show thread coming up (↑) or going down (↓) into fabric. Where thread does not show on top, it will show on the back.

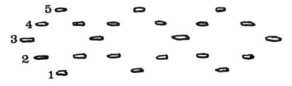

Diamonds

Man

Horse

Cactus

A.11 FLAT STITCH AND FILLING
Croatian Flat Stitch

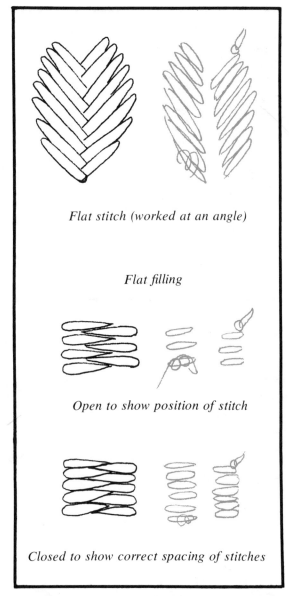

Flat stitch (worked at an angle)

Flat filling

Open to show position of stitch

Closed to show correct spacing of stitches

RHYTHM
Up / down–angle up to right–up / down–angle up to left–up /

USES
Wide borders, rectangular areas, leaf shapes and filling.

REMARKS
A very friendly stitch. Easy to catch the rhythm as it falls into place readily. Covers very well.

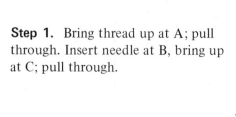

D.O.W. ↓

Step 1. Bring thread up at A; pull through. Insert needle at B, bring up at C; pull through.

Step 2. Insert needle at D, bring up at E; pull through.

Step 3. Continue until space is covered. The lower part of each new stitch will cover the end of the previous stitch, giving an interlocking effect.

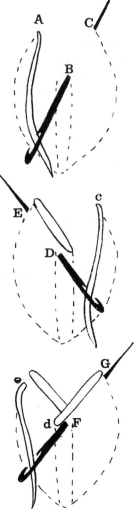

The only difference between working the flat filling and leaf-shaped filling is that the needle is slanted for the leaf shape (above) and it is held straight across for the diagram on the right. Several rows are worked side by side in larger areas.

RHYTHM

Up / down–up / turn down–short up /

USES

Very wide borders, large geometric area filling. Use this stitch in place of satin stitch when space to be covered is too wide for one stitch to span.

REMARKS

This stitch is worked best in heavy thread. It covers large areas very quickly and is easy to keep even. Do not use it if area should be shaded.

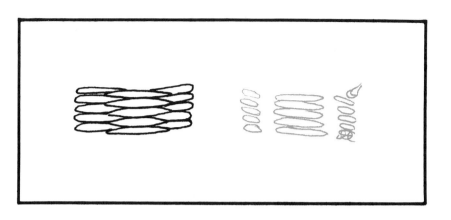

Step 1. Bring thread up at A; pull through. Insert needle at B, bring out at C and pull through. (L = Left, CL = Center Left, RC = Center Right, R = Right.)

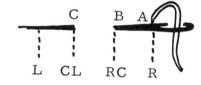

Step 2. Insert needle at D, bring out at E (just left of CL and close to the stitch D-C) and pull through.

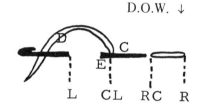

Step 3. Insert needle at F (just right of RC and very close to stitch B-A). Bring out at G and pull through.

Step 4. Insert needle at H (on RC line and very close to stitch above) and bring out at I. Pull through.

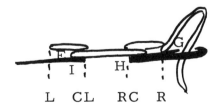

A.13 ODD SPOKE STITCH

Spoke Stitch, Wheel Stitch

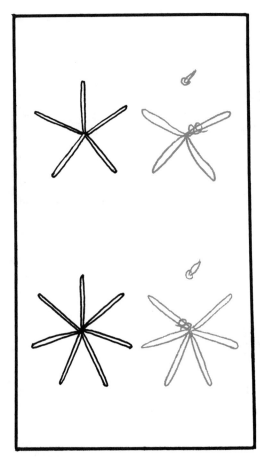

D.O.W. Any

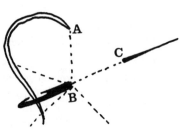

Step 1. Bring needle out at A; pull through. Insert needle at B, bring out at C; pull through.

Step 2. Insert needle again at B, bring out at D and pull through. Continue until all spokes have been covered.

Step 3. Finish by bringing working thread to back of work and knotting off securely.

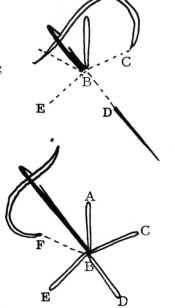

RHYTHM
Up / down in center, up at end of spoke /

USES
Five-pointed stars, basis for whipping or decorating. Use many tiny stars as a scattered filling.

REMARKS
An odd number are required when used as a basis for circular weaving (see woven spoke, J.1). If you need an even number of spokes, it is easier to work the traditional spoke or star cross stitch (F.2). The knot is placed at the end of one of the spokes so that you won't have to push it aside each time you go down into the center.

RHYTHM
Up / down–up at end of spoke /

USES
Very decorative isolated stitch, easily worked. Use as a center of interest or line up as a side border stitch.

REMARKS
To keep uniform, work on the straight of the fabric, following a thread of the material to line each stitch up evenly. When working freehand, work verticals in a straight line, then horizontals crossing the center at perfect right angles. Then fill in the stitches between, dividing each right angle evenly in half.

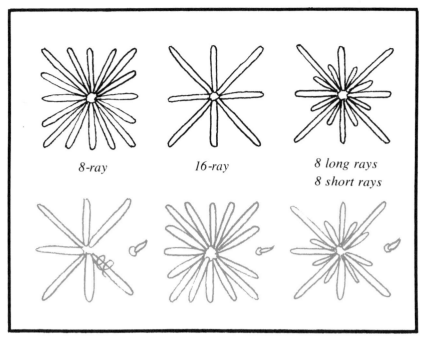

8-ray   *16-ray*   *8 long rays*
                                    8 short rays

D.O.W. ↘→

Step 1. Bring thread up at A; pull through. Insert needle at center of square (B), bring up at C and pull through.

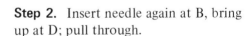

Step 2. Insert needle again at B, bring up at D; pull through.

Step 3. Insert needle again at B, bring up at E; pull through.

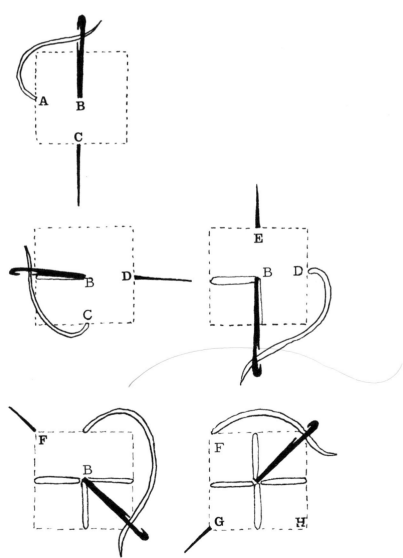

Step 4. Insert needle again at B, bring up at F; pull through.

Step 5. Continue inserting needle at center (B) and bring it up at each corner until star is completed.

Note

For 16 rays work a straight stitch between each of the original 8, always inserting needle at center. A second color may be used for last 8 stitches.

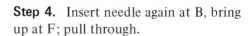

17

A.15 FERN STITCH

RHYTHM

Up / down–angle up to the right–up / down in same hole–angle up to left–up / down–straight up /

USES

Feathery leaves or stems.

REMARKS

Although pretty just as it is, this stitch can be decorated to form a graceful branching flower. Group French knots or daisy stitches in a circle at the end of each branch.

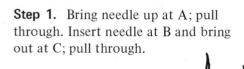

Step 1. Bring needle up at A; pull through. Insert needle at B and bring out at C; pull through.

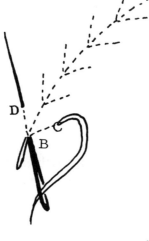

Step 2. Insert needle again at B, bring out at D; pull through.

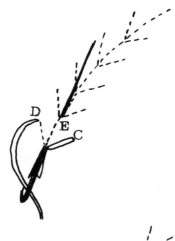

Step 3. Insert needle again at B, bring out at E; pull through.

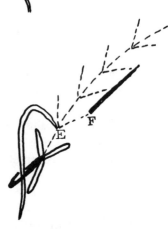

Step 4. Insert needle again at B, bring out at F; pull through.

SINGLE LACED RUNNING STITCH

Set row of running stitches in first, working stitches evenly and so that each stitch is three times as long as the space between stitches. Lace through in manner shown; do not pierce fabric until end. Insert needle at B, pull through to back and knot off. Do not pull lacing too tightly.

DOUBLE LACED RUNNING STITCH

Follow instructions for single lacing (above) but do not pull through to the back at B. Lace back to the beginning in opposite direction, making sure needle goes under both stitch and first lacing. Insert at A, pull through to back, and knot off.

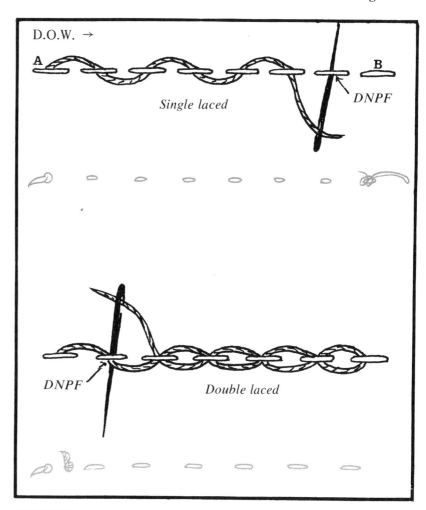

D.O.W. →

A   B   *Single laced*   DNPF

DNPF   *Double laced*

RHYTHM
(Lacing only) up / over down / over up /

USES
Thin line stitch that is quick and easy; ideal for stems, outlining an area; makes a very interesting pattern when repeated to fill an area.

REMARKS
Remember, lacing does not pierce fabric except at beginning and end. When the thread is above the running stitch, come down from above; when below, go back up from below. Use a dull-pointed tapestry needle for lacing to avoid splitting base threads, or insert crewel needle eye-end first.

Looks like chain stitch with a back stitch when double laced. Try lacing other stitches such as chains, arrowheads, back stitch etc.

A.17 WHIPPED RUNNING STITCH

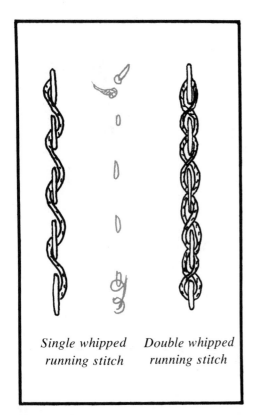

Single whipped
running stitch

Double whipped
running stitch

RHYTHM
Up on left / slide under from right / continue, always from right.

USES
Lines, borders, outlining areas, stems.

REMARKS
Single and double whipping always slides from the same side.

Whipping will cover the space between the basic running stitches so that a stamped design will be completely covered.

Use a dull-pointed tapestry needle for lacing to avoid splitting base threads, or insert crewel needle eye-end first.

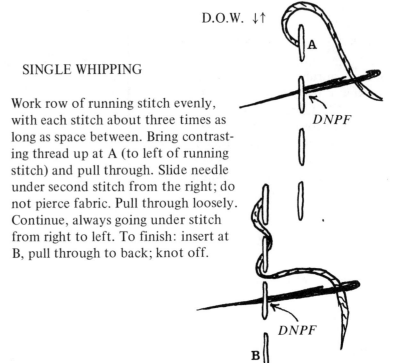

D.O.W. ↓↑

SINGLE WHIPPING

Work row of running stitch evenly, with each stitch about three times as long as space between. Bring contrasting thread up at A (to left of running stitch) and pull through. Slide needle under second stitch from the right; do not pierce fabric. Pull through loosely. Continue, always going under stitch from right to left. To finish: insert at B, pull through to back; knot off.

DOUBLE WHIPPING

Work single whip first, but do not end at B. Slide needle under both threads (second stitch from bottom) and pull through. This forms a figure eight. Continue working, always from right to left to the end. Insert needle at A, to the right of the running stitch, pull through and knot off.

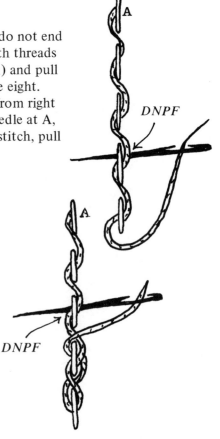

D.O.W. ↑

Step 1. Work parallel rows of running stitch. Bring contrasting thread up at A (to the right of stitch) and slide needle under second stitch on right. Pull through; do not pierce fabric.

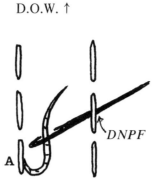

DNPF

Step 2. Slide needle under first stitch, over lacing and under second stitch on left side. Pull through.

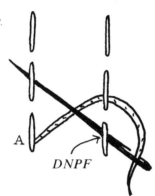

DNPF

Step 3. Slide needle under first running stitch on left, over lacing, and under third stitch on right. Pull through.

DNPF

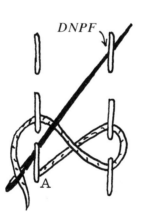

Step 4. Slide needle under second stitch on right, over lacing, and under third stitch on left. Continue in this manner to top. End by inserting needle under last stitch near the middle; pull through and knot off.

DNPF

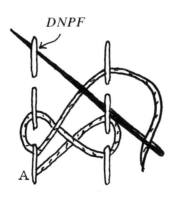

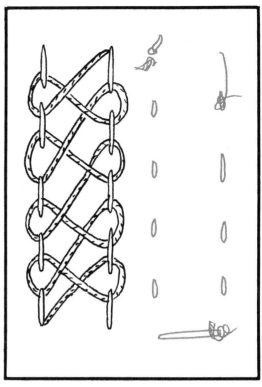

RHYTHM
Cross over to next stitch from inside / down and back on outside to previous stitch / cross over to new stitch on other side and slide from inside.

COMPOSITION
Parallel rows of running stitch with back lacing.

USES
Wide decorative borders, great for Jacobean tree trunks.

REMARKS
This interweaving can be worked on a Holbein or back stitch base. It will give a more solid effect on the edges. Try staggering base stitches on each side so that angle of lacing increases; this makes an interesting pattern.

Use a dull-pointed tapestry needle for lacing to avoid splitting base threads, or insert crewel needle eye-end first.

A.19 CLOUD FILLING STITCH

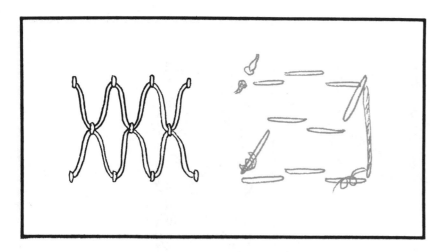

RHYTHM
Up / under–line below slide / line above slide /

USES
Light filling; covers large area quickly.

REMARKS
Keep tension loose in lacing. This will allow a graceful curve to develop in the lacing. Each center (diamond shape) may be filled with isolated stitches, such as French knots, to further decorate. Use a dull-pointed tapestry needle for lacing to avoid splitting base threads or insert crewel needle eye-end first.

D.O.W. →

Step 1. Lay foundation of tiny vertical straight stitches. Notice that alternate rows are staggered in a brick pattern. Bring thread up at A, pull through; do not pierce fabric. Slide needle from left to right under first straight stitch on top line; pull through. Slide under first stitch on second line; pull through; then up to the top line again. Continue until first two lines are filled.

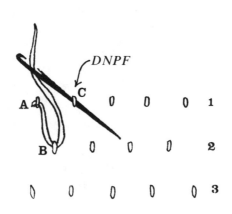

Step 2. Work same as Step 1 but in rows 2 and 3. Although this row is shown being worked from left to right, it may be worked from right to left equally well. The needle would then go through from right to left.

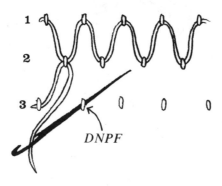

family **B**

BACK STITCHES

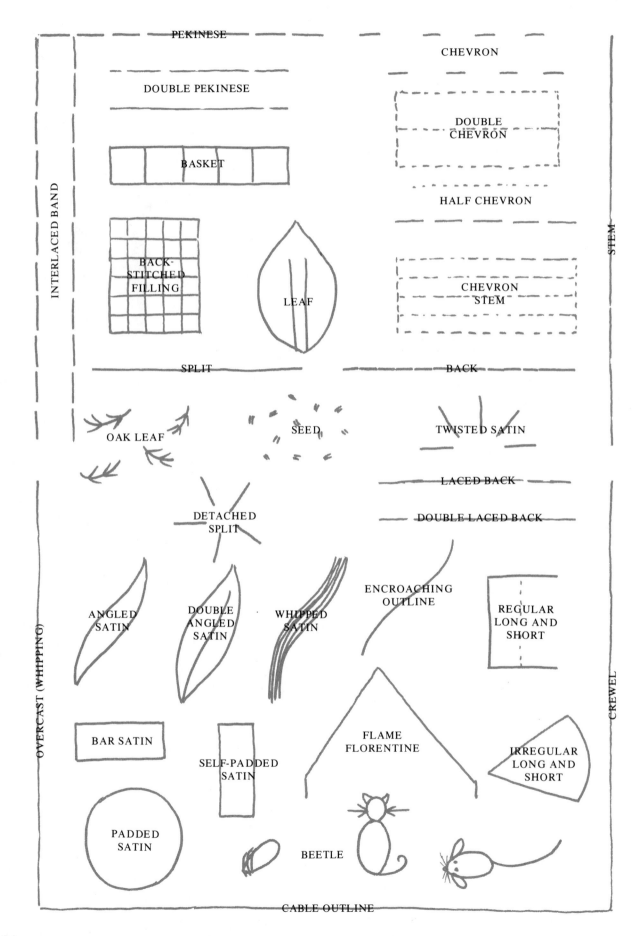

family B Back Stitches

Basic rhythm: down and up, encircling motion   ↑ /𝒢𝒶𝓍𝓍𝓍

Progression of difficulty

Isolated (Basic Stitch) 1. SEED (Isolated Back)
  2. DETACHED SPLIT (Swedish Split)
  3. OAK LEAF
  4. TWISTED SATIN

Line 5. BACK
  6. STEM (Outline)
  7. CREWEL
  8. CABLE OUTLINE
  9. SPLIT

Angled 10. ANGLED SATIN (Slanted Satin)

Stacked 11. STACKED OUTLINE (Encroaching Outline, Encroaching Stem)
  12. REGULAR LONG AND SHORT (Brick)
  13. LONG AND SHORT (Irregular)
  14. BAR SATIN (Padded Satin)
  15. PATTERNED SATIN (Flame, Florentine)
  16. BEETLE
  17. LEAF

Grouped 18. BASKET (Basket Satin, Basket Filling)
  19. CHEVRON (Double Chevron, Chevron Filling)
  20. HALF-CHEVRON
  21. BACK-STITCHED FILLING

Combined 22. OVERCAST (Whipping)
  23. PEKINESE
  24. DOUBLE PEKINESE (Double Back-laced Back)
  25. LACED BACK (Threaded Back)
  26. INTERLACED BAND (Parallel Line Whipping)
  27. WHIPPED SATIN
  28. CHEVRON STEM (Raised Zig-zag Stem)

B.1 SEED STITCH
Isolated Back Stitch

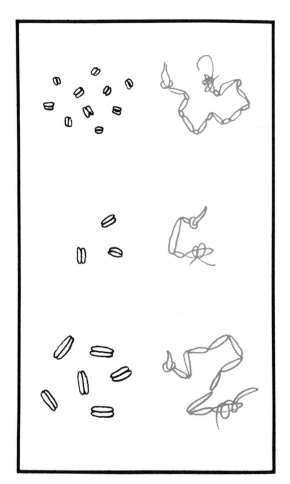

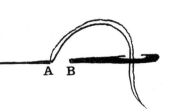

Step 1. Bring thread up at A, pull through. Insert needle at B and bring up again at A; pull through.

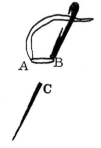

Step 2. Insert needle at B. Pull through to back to complete first stitch. However, needle may be brought up at C to start next stitch before it is pulled through.

Note

Using the "stab" method may take longer to work but it is more accurate in placing stitches evenly. Stitches should be evenly spaced and of equal length but direction of each should vary. Do not form a regular pattern.

RHYTHM
Up / down / up first hole / down second hole /
USES
Light powdery filling; use on "hills" in Jacobean designs to give light shading or to partially shade in flowers.

REMARKS
Note similarity to "quilt knot" (see G.18). Only difference is that two long ends are left standing loose on top of fabric in quilt knot. This is also called "turkey work" when closely packed.

D.O.W. Any

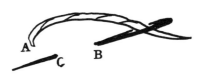

Step 1. Using double thread twisted in needle, bring thread up at A; pull through. Insert at B and bring up at C; pull through.

Step 2. Insert needle into stitch A-B so that threads are split equally. Pull through.

ANOTHER METHOD

Step 1. Using double thread in needle bring up at A; pull through. Insert needle at B, bring up at C splitting the thread in half, and pull through.

Step 2. Insert needle at D, very close to stitch A-B, bring up at E (to start another stitch) and pull through. Split stitch (see B.9) may also be worked with this method.

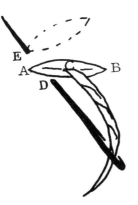

RHYTHM
Up / down—up / split down / up
USES
Use as a scattered filling stitch, arrange in a circle as a flower, or along a stem as leaves.

REMARKS
The ''stab'' method may be used for this stitch to great advantage. For variation, try placing all straight stitches first, then, with another color, place all splitting stitches.

B.3 OAK LEAF STITCH

Enlarged

Actual size

D.O.W. Any

Step 1. Bring thread up at A; pull through. Insert needle at B, bring up at C, pull through loosely.

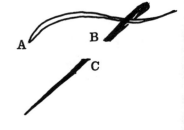

Step 2. With point of needle through thread only at D, drag stitch A-B down slightly to form a gentle curve, then pierce fabric. Bring needle up at E and pull through.

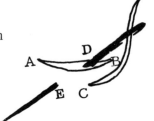

Step 3. Again drag stitch A-B down to complete the curve by inserting needle at F through thread only. Then pierce fabric, bring up at G and pull through.

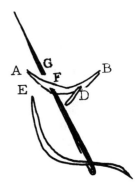

RHYTHM
Up / down—up / push into curve—split down /

USES
Light filling, attach to stem for leaves.

REMARKS
A very useful stitch in free form stitchery because no diagram is needed; just scatter the leaves at random. Oak leaves turn a lovely russet brown in the fall.

Steps 4 and 5. Insert needle again at F, bring out at H, pull through. Insert needle again at D, pull through and end off.

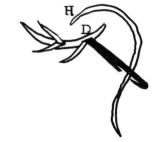

D.O.W. Any

Step 1. Bring thread up at A; pull through. Insert needle at B, bring up again at A; pull through.

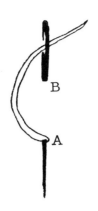

Step 2. Slide needle under stitch A-B and pull through. Do not pierce fabric.

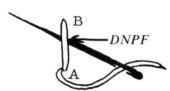 *—DNPF*

Step 3. Insert needle again at B. Bring up to start a new stitch or pull through to the back to finish.

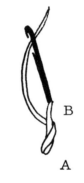

RHYTHM
Up / down—up / same as first / slide / down same as second

USES
As a scattered filling, arranged in a wheel to form a flower or in a trio to form a bud.

REMARKS
This stitch looks better when worked in heavy yarn (like worsted) or in a double crewel yarn.

B.5 BACK STITCH

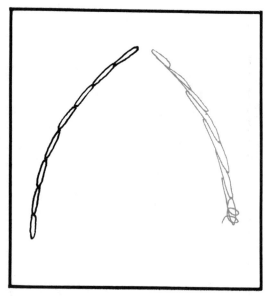

Step 1. Bring thread up at A; pull through. Insert needle at B and bring up at C; pull through.

D.O.W. ←

Step 2. Insert needle again at B, bring out at D and pull through.

RHYTHM
Up / over one space—down—under one space—up / back in last hole down—under two spaces—up /

USES
Fine lines, outlining, tiny stems and tendrils.

REMARKS
Back stitch is the back of the outline stitch. It follows a tight curve very well if the stitches are kept tiny. It is the base stitch for many other stitches: see Pekinese, interlaced band, etc.

Back stitch may be combined with many other stitches to produce special effects. For example: Work chain stitch first and then, with contrasting color, work back stitch into the center of each loop; you have chained back stitch! Or work large back stitches and then whip with contrasting color for whipped back stitch.

Note

Stitches should be small, evenly spaced and regular. When working a sharply curved line, stitches should be very tiny, so that curve flows—no sharp angles. Be sure to place each stitch in the same hole at the end of the pre- ceeding one. Stitch should look like machine stitching. It will also look like the back of outline stitch.

Step 1.   Bring thread up at A; pull through. Insert needle at B and bring up at C (about half the distance from A to B and on the same line). Holding the yarn below the line, pull through.

D.O.W. →

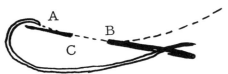

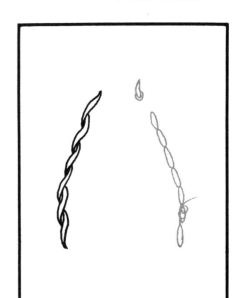

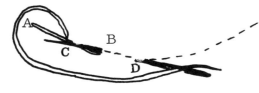

Step 2.   Holding thread below the line, insert needle at D and bring up at B (at right end of previous stitch and in the same hole). Pull through. Continue to end of line, making sure thread is always held below the line.

Note

The stem stitch is most frequently used for narrow, curving lines. When curve is in the opposite direction, thread may be held always above the line.

Diagram shows stitches greatly enlarged. They should be tiny, especially on a sharp curve.

RHYTHM
Up / thread below—over two spaces —down—back under 1 space—up /

USES
Outlining any area, stems.

REMARKS
By working parallel row upon row, this becomes a very solid filling stitch which is easily shaded.

Outline stitch is frequently used with another stitch to define edges, accent, etc. For example, mark a leaf pattern in satin stitch and then outline outside edges with lighter or darker shades for contrast.

B.7 CREWEL STITCH

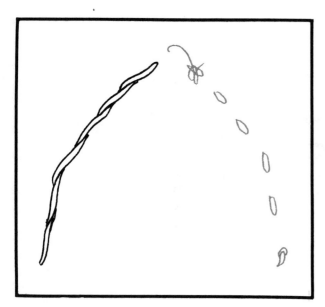

RHYTHM
Up / hold thread above—over two spaces down—back half a space—up / thread above /

USES
Thin line, outlining.

REMARKS
Crewel stitch works faster than outline, does not have to be as accurate, is a bit longer and looser and is thinner in coverage. When stacked, row upon row, this makes an excellent filling stitch, especially when shading needs to run the length of the design.

Step 1. Bring thread up at A; pull through. Always holding thread above the line, insert needle at B, bring up at C; pull through.   D.O.W. →

Step 2. Holding thread above the line, insert needle at D, bring up at E; pull through.

Note

Crewel stitch is a variation of outline (stem) stitch. The difference is that only a small stitch is picked up to overlap the previous stitch instead of beginning the third stitch at the end of the first.

Thread may be held always under the line rather than always above, but must be consistent.

RHYTHM
Up / thread below—over two spaces—down—back one space—up / thread above, etc.

USES
Slightly heavier line than outline stitch.

REMARKS
Well controlled, looks like two close rows of back stitch. This stitch is also used in smocking as a gathering stitch. It is pulled up tight, thus puckering the fabric.

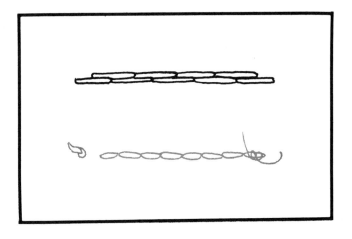

D.O.W. ←

Step 1. Bring thread up at A; pull through. Holding thread below the line, insert needle at B, bring up at C and pull through.

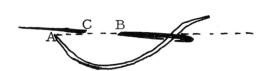

Step 2. Holding thread above the line, insert needle at D and bring up at B (same hole at right end of A-B stitch) and pull through.

Step 3. Holding thread below the line, insert needle at E, bring up at D, pull through. Continue, holding thread above and then below line when working following stitches.

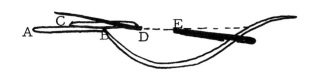

B.9 SPLIT STITCH

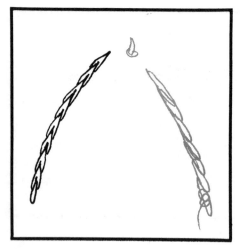

RHYTHM

Up / over one space down—under one space up / back one and a half spaces—split thread—down under two spaces—up /

USES

Covers line; wider than outline stitch but narrower than chain stitch.

REMARKS

Looks like a tiny chain stitch. Good on fine stems, tightly curved. Most directions for working split stitch call for splitting the stitch from below as the needle comes up through the fabric. I find this method much more difficult, but try it to see which method you like better!

Step 1. Bring thread up at A; pull through. Insert needle at B and bring out at C, making space between C and B about half as long as space between B and A. Pull through.

D.O.W. ←

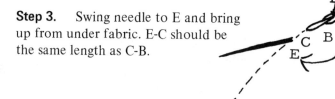

Step 2. Pointing needle straight down, insert needle into stitch B-A, splitting thread in half.

Step 3. Swing needle to E and bring up from under fabric. E-C should be the same length as C-B.

D.O.W. ↑

Step 1.   Bring thread up at A; pull through. Insert needle at B, bring out at C, pull through.

Step 2.   Insert needle at D, very close to B, bring up at E, keeping a wider space between C and E than between B and D. This will keep the stitches at a pretty angle. Do not crowd stitches. Do not pull up too tightly.

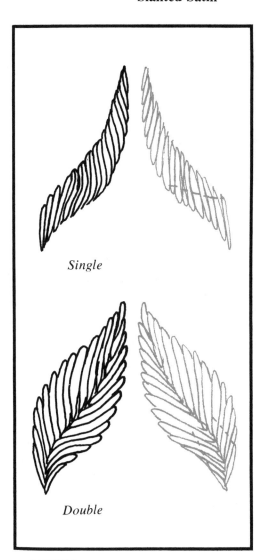

Single

Double

DOUBLE SATIN

Work as for single area. Needle sketched in dotted lines) shows angle at which first half was worked. The working thread should always come up on the outside of the leaf design, and the needle be inserted on the center line.

To work second half, (usually in a different shade) bring thread up at A; pull through. Insert at B, bring up at C; pull through. Insert at D, very close to B and in the same hole right-hand stitches were worked. Continue, maintaining slant. To finish off at end, bring thread to the back and weave in.

RHYTHM
Up / down—up /

USES
Solid filling in leaves, petals, etc.

REMARKS
Threads should completely cover fabric, but do not crowd in too many stitches, which will make the leaf look thick and ugly. If you can keep the V-shape in the center, all stitches will be long enough to fall gracefully in place and you will avoid the short, flat stiches at the tip of the leaf which make an ugly bump!

B.11 STACKED OUTLINE STITCH
Encroaching Outline, Encroaching Stem Stitch

RHYTHM
Up / down—up /

USES
Filling shaded areas, flowers and leaves, folds of material (as in a flag).

REMARKS
When shading must follow along on a line, as in folds in fabric, use this stitch in rows, one shade following a line and the next shade worked directly above or below. Remember to use dark shades deep inside folds or at bottom of areas and light shades towards top. Weave thread in to start and stop this stitch. Do not knot!

FIRST ROW

Step 1.   As if to work outline stitch, insert needle slightly away from the line. Holding thread above the line, after bringing thread up at A and pulling through, insert needle at B, bring up at C, and pull through.

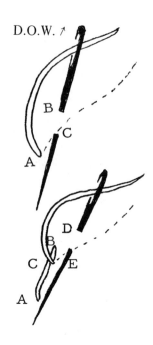

Step 2.   Always holding thread above line, continue placing slanting stitches until line is covered.

SECOND ROW

Turn work around. Bring thread up at AA and pull through. Drag needle back between first and second stitch, almost to line; insert needle at BB, bring out at CC and pull through. Continue to end.

Note

Each row, when worked in a different color or shade, makes a beautiful shading effect.

D.O.W. Any

Step 1. Bring thread up at A; pull through. Insert at B and bring out at C; pull through. This makes the long stitch and starts the short one.

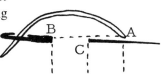

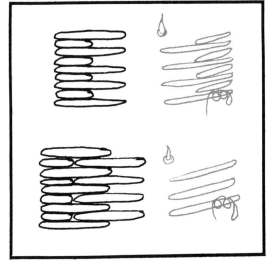

Step 2. Insert needle at D, right next to B, and bring out at E, leaving one thread space between A and E; pull through.

Step 3. Insert needle at F, bring out at G; pull through.

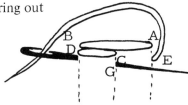

RHYTHM
Up / down—up /

USES
Solid filling.

REMARKS
Use this stitch for even, smooth covering of an area. Works best on geometric shapes—square, rectangular, etc.

Note

All short stitches will be the same length and all long stitches will be the same length. When continuing this stitch, *after first journey, all stitches are long and every other one is worked in each successive journey.*

When used to fill an irregular space, it is best to work center stitch first, then complete upper stitches, then lower.

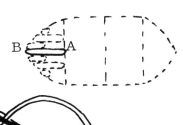

Add additional stitches to outside edges of area as needed.

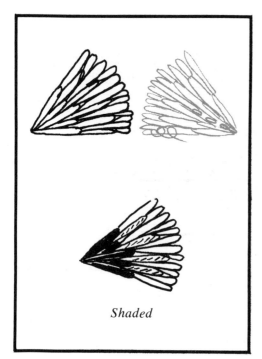

Shaded

RHYTHM
Up / down—up /

USES
Solid filling; probably used more than any other stitch to fill large areas completely. It is easily shaded.

REMARKS
Here are some tricks to make work easier:

After first row of long and short stitches, all stitches will be long, and some longer (uneven in length). Avoid too short stitches because they make work look bumpy.

Do not leave gaps where fabric shows through, but do not pack in too many stitches.

Notice that thread is always outside of finished area, and needle drags between previous stitches before insertion through fabric.

D.O.W. Any   Many Journeys

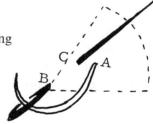

Step 1.   Weave end in (no knot). Bring thread out at A; pull through. Insert needle at B and bring up at C, pull through.

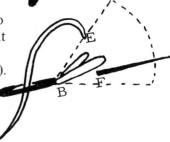

Step 2.   Push stitch B-A down and insert needle at D, bring up at E and pull through.

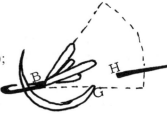

Step 3.   Insert needle again at B (to keep point) and bring up at F, so that this short stitch will be about the same length as first short stitch (D-C).

Steps 4 and 5.   Complete short stitch (G-F) using Step 2, but push B-A up. Insert needle again at B and bring up at H (to start second journey); pull through.

Steps 6 and 7.   Drag point of needle between stitches of first journey; do not use same holes as stitches before. All stitches will be long, but try to avoid making them equal in length. Variety makes for better shading. Never cross stitches; if you are not sure on which side a new stitch should be placed, hold working thread on either side of old stitch to see how it will lie when completed.

Note

After each journey (or two) is completed, change to another shade of the same color to effect smooth, gradual change of shading.

D.O.W. Any

Step 1. Bring thread up at A; pull through. Insert needle at B, bring up at C very close to A; pull through.

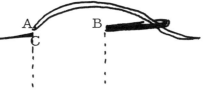

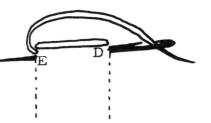

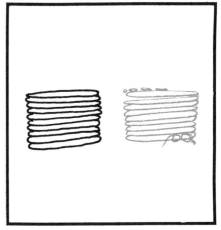

Step 2. Insert needle at D, bring up at E; pull through. Continue, keeping stitches even in length and lying so closely together that no fabric shows through. End off by weaving in on the back side.

RHYTHM
Up / down—up / (whipping motion)
USES
Solid filling, monogramming.
REMARKS
Bar satin covers even, geometric areas nicely. Do not use for leaves; the short stitches at the pointed end are bumpy and unattractive. Many flower shapes and especially centers are most attractive when padded.

SELF-PADDED SATIN

Work long satin stitches first, then cover with satin stitches worked across. This gives a thick, padded effect.

Area may be outlined first with stem stitch, split stitch, chain stitch, running stitch, etc., to pad only the outer edge. Or entirely fill the area with any of these stitches to pad completely. (The diagrams are only partially worked to show padding. When completed, only top satin will show.)

B.15 PATTERNED SATIN
Flame Stitch, Florentine Stitch

Note

See regular long and short (brick) stitch for working method (B.12).

D.O.W. ⇄   Many Journeys

Satin stitches (all the same length) are arranged in regular, repeating patterns. This stitch is most easily done on a regular (even) weave fabric, with threads counted to assure evenness of stitch and spacing. Although here the shading is worked across from top to bottom, the flame effect may be worked by carrying one color up one side and down the other.

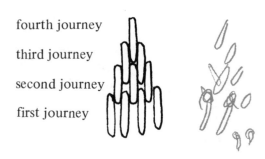

fourth journey

third journey

second journey

first journey

There are many variations of this stitch, both in arrangement of stitches and shading. They may be worked solidly or with open spaces left between. It is most effective when design is repeated many times.

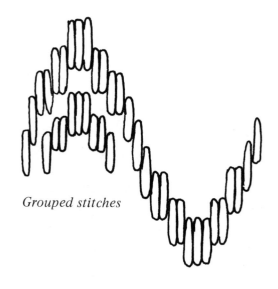

Grouped stitches

RHYTHM
Up / down—up /

USES
Wide borders, filling.

REMARKS
Patterns follow an up-and-down flow. Grouping may differ, but a regular pattern remains throughout the work.

Step 1.   Using two threads in needle, bring needle up at A; pull through. Insert needle at B and bring out again at A; pull through.

D.O.W. Any

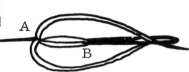

Step 2.   Insert needle again at B, bring out at A; pull through. Threads will sometimes separate (as shown); this helps to build up sides evenly. Repeat four to six times or until a fat, padded ball is formed. As stitch grows, it is easier to use stab method to place successive stitches.

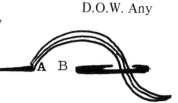

1   2   3

RHYTHM
Up / down—up same hole /

USES
Any padded, raised small circular or oval area.

REMARKS
The beetle stitch can be as varied as your imagination allows. If a cat and mouse are possible, how about a turtle? Have fun!

This is a fun stitch! Work it in red to make a ladybug (1), add gold dot stitch spots, black French knot eyes and (with black cotton sewing thread) add straight stitch legs. Or, with soft gray yarn, make pussy-willows (2), then add a cup with satin stitch in rust slanted over the base. Add these, alternating, to a twig of stem stitch in rust.

Or even a mouse (3)! Ears are lazy daisy stitches, eyes are black French knots, tail is outline stitch. Whiskers are black sewing thread—just straight stitches.

B.17 LEAF STITCH

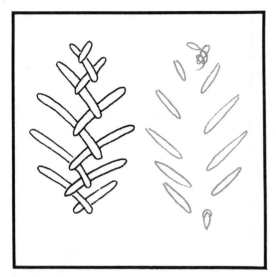

RHYTHM
Up / thread above—down—up / (angle right —angle left)

USES
Filling leaf shapes.

REMARKS
If you picture outline stitch being stacked up instead of running along in a line, it will help you with the rhythm.

Step 1. Bring thread up at A; pull through. Holding thread always above the needle, insert at B, bring up at C; pull through.

D.O.W. ↑

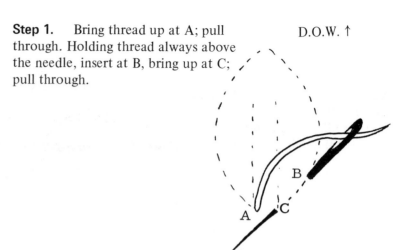

Step 2. Insert needle at D, bring up at E; pull through.

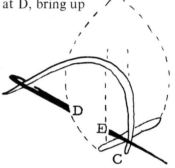

Step 3. Continue until leaf shape is formed. Stitch will slant more and become shorter as the top of the leaf is shaped.

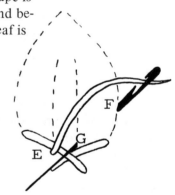

Note

This stitch is usually worked very openly, leaving a printed line still showing. The outside may be covered by working outline stitch or back stitch over this line.

Steps 1 - 3.   Bring thread up at A; pull through. Insert needle at B, bring up at C (close to A) and pull through. Continue until four straight stitches are formed, all equal in length and laid close together.

D.O.W. ↓ and →

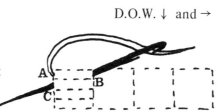

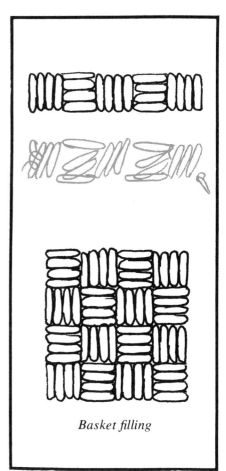

Steps 4 - 7.   Continue making stitches of equal length but lay them at right angles to first group. Continue until area is covered, all even squares having horizontal stitches, all odd squares vertical. Work opposite direction for each row of filling stitch.

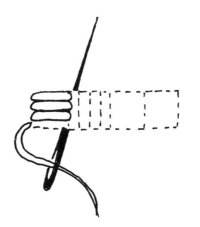

Basket filling

RHYTHM
Up / down—up / (square in one direction, then square in other)

USES
Filling or borders.

REMARKS
Although this stitch may be worked in one color, it is very attractive when a second color is used for alternating blocks—as in a chess board.

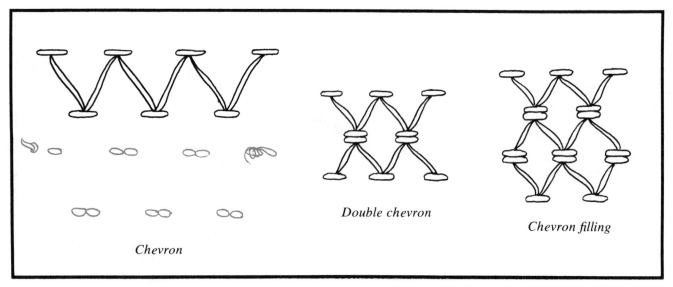

Chevron

Double chevron

Chevron filling

D.O.W. →

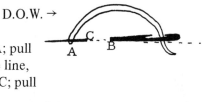

Step 1.   Bring thread up at A; pull through. Holding thread above line, insert needle at B, bring up at C; pull through.

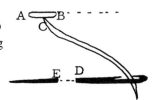

Step 2.   Insert needle at D, bring up at E; pull through. (E-D is half as long as A-B, and point E, on lower line, is directly below B.)

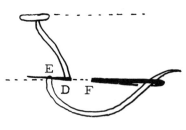

Step 3.   Holding thread below line, insert needle at F, bring up at D (same hole) and pull through.

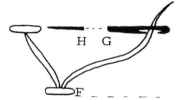

Step 4.   Holding thread below line, insert needle at G, bring up at H; pull through.

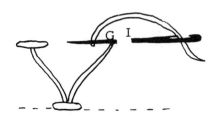

Step 5.   Same as Step 1. Continue until line is covered.

RHYTHM
Up / thread above—down, halfway back—up / lower line—thread above —down—up / thread below—down —halfway back—up same hole /

USES
Borders, filling.

REMARKS
This is the basic smocking (gathering) stitch.

Note

To work double chevron and chevron filling, a second row is worked directly below the first, etc. When this stitch is used for smocking, stitches A-B, E-F, etc. are pulled up tightly, puckering the material.

RHYTHM
Up / thread below—down—up / thread to the
right—down—up /

USES
Wide borders.

REMARKS
This stitch combines outline stitch below with
faggoting stitch above. Looks best when worked
very evenly.

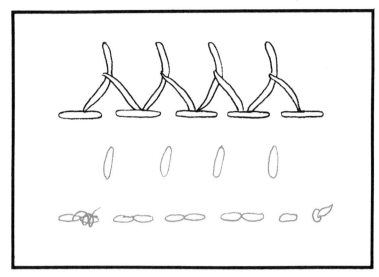

D.O.W. →

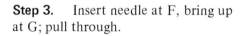

Step 1.   Bring thread up at A; pull
through. Holding thread below the
line, insert needle at B, bring up at C;
pull through.

Step 2.   Holding the thread to the
right, insert needle at D and bring up
at E; pull through.

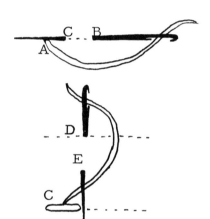

Step 3.   Insert needle at F, bring up
at G; pull through.

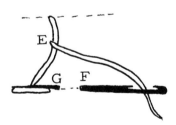

Step 4.   Holding thread below line,
insert needle at E, bring up at F, (same
hole) and pull through.

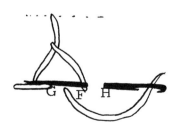

45

B.21 BACK-STITCHED FILLING

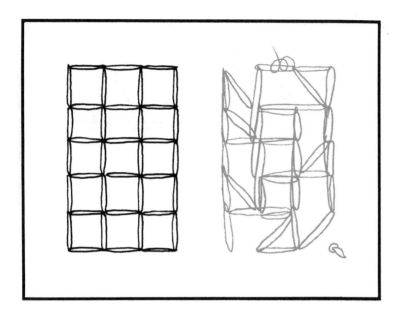

RHYTHM
Up / over one space—down—under one space—up / back and down into same hole —under two spaces—up /

USES
Light filling.

REMARKS
The back of this stitch looks like a rat's nest. If this design is used on a table cloth, for example, where both sides may be seen, use Holbein filling stitch, which is the same on both sides.

See working method for back stitch (B.5).

D.O.W. ↗↘ 2 Journeys

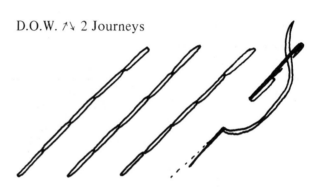

Step 1. Using back stitch, work all parallel lines in one direction to cover area. Keep spacing regular. Work on one straight thread of the fabric, if possible, to help keep stitches even.

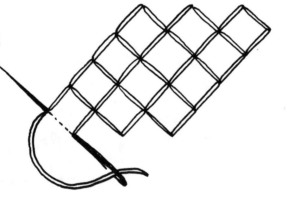

Step 2. Using back stitch, work all perpendicular rows, until area is covered. Be sure stitch is formed in the same hole in which previous stitch was worked.

A diamond effect may be achieved by working the second group of rows on a bias, slanting.

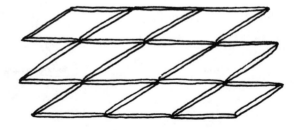

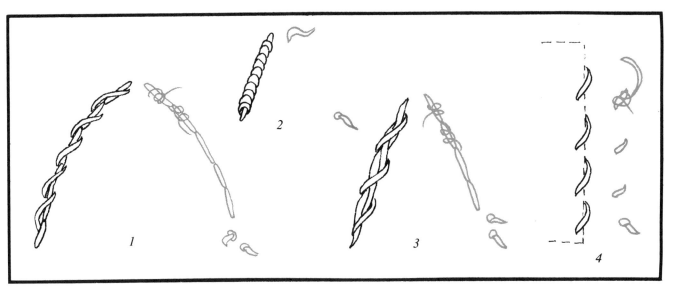

Step 1.   Lay foundation stitches. Many are suitable including running, back, outline, chain, etc. Here back stitch is shown. Bring thread up at A; pull through. Slide needle under second stitch and pull through; do not pierce fabric.

Step 2.   Continue, whipping each stitch until all are covered. (1)

VARIATIONS

One long stitch is whipped until completely filled (2).

Whipping over outline stitch gives a heavier line (3).

Whipping (overcasting) along edge of fabric to prevent raveling (4).

Note

An attractive edge for a free-standing wall hanging may be made by raveling the threads along the sides until an inch or so of warp threads are free. Save the threads to overcast the edge where raveling stops. These threads may also be used to twist into a rope for hanging the finished work on a dowel or curtain rod.

D.O.W. Any

<-- - - *DNPF*

A

RHYTHM
Up / slide under /

USES
To decorate any stitch, to overcast raw edges.

REMARKS
Almost any stitch may be overcast or whipped. Try a variety of color combinations.

47

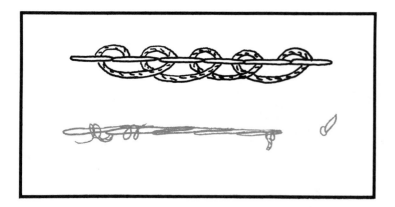

RHYTHM
(Lacing only) Up top of second stitch / back—slide under from top to complete first stitch / skip second—slide under third from below /
USES
Chinese embroidery uses it, row upon row, as a shaded filling stitch; also good for wide borders.
REMARKS
Remember that when thread is on top of the line, go back to complete previous stitch. When thread is below, skip and move to new stitch.

Note

Work foundation of large, evenly spaced back stitch or Holbein stitch.

Step 1.   Bring thread up at A, near left end and above second stitch, so that hole at A is hidden beneath second stitch; pull through. Slide needle under first stitch, from top to bottom (do not pierce fabric) and pull through loosely.

Step 2.   Slide needle under third stitch from bottom to top (do not pierce fabric) and pull through loosely.

Step 3.   Go back to second stitch, slide needle from top to bottom under both stitch and threading, and pull through loosely.

Continue to end. Finish by inserting needle at right end of second stitch from the end, so that end will be hidden by that stitch.

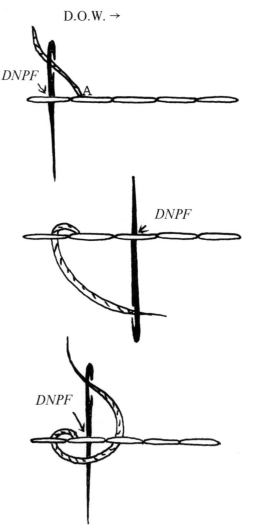

Note

Work foundation of back stitch (two parallel rows) one-half to one inch apart. See working method, B.5.

D.O.W. ↑

Step 1.   Bring thread up at A, so that hole at A is hidden by first stitch on bottom of left row. Slide needle from left to right under second stitch on right row; do not pierce fabric. Pull through.

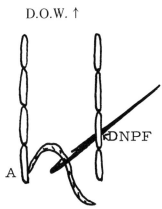

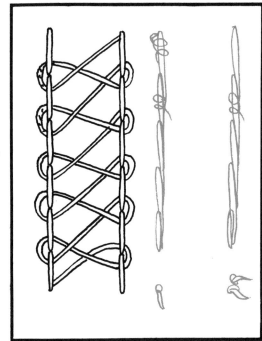

Step 2.   Slide needle under first stitch on right row from right to left. Pass over threading, under second stitch on left row, pull through loosely.

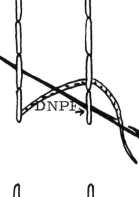

RHYTHM
(Lacing only) Cross over inside to new stitch. When on outside, go back to stitch before to complete.

USES
Wide border stitch, great for Jacobean tree trunks and branches.

REMARKS
Try staggering foundation back stitches; the lacing will then have quite a slant and will produce an interesting effect in crewel work.

Step 3.   Slide needle under first stitch, over threading and under third stitch. Pull through. Continue until all back stitches have been laced. End by inserting needle under last stitch so that end is hidden.

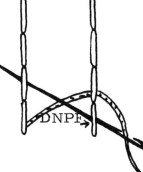

49

B.25 LACED BACK STITCH
Threaded Back Stitch

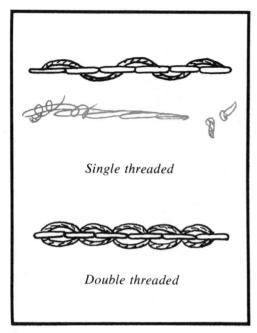

Single threaded

Double threaded

RHYTHM

Up / from top to top of next—slide / from bottom to bottom—slide /

USES

Narrow borders.

REMARKS

Many stitches may be laced; try some chains and feathers. Remember, when lacing, thread goes back and forth beneath stitch but does not cross over top of foundation stitches. (That would be whipping.)

Step 1.   Work foundation of back stitch. With contrasting thread, bring needle up at A and pull through. Slide needle under second stitch, from top to bottom. Do not pierce fabric. Pull up loosely.

D.O.W. →

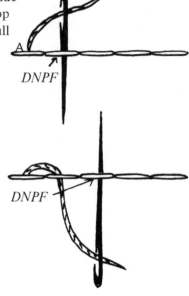

Step 2.   Slide needle under third stitch from bottom to top; do not pierce fabric; pull up loosely. Continue to end.

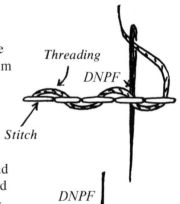

DOUBLE THREADED

Step 1.   After single threading, slide needle under stitch and threading from top to bottom at second stitch from the right end. Do not pierce fabric.

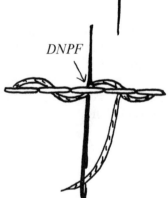

Step 2.   Slide needle under stitch and threading from bottom to top of third stitch. Continue to end. To finish, insert needle again at A from below first stitch. Pull through, knot off.

RHYTHM
(Whipping only) Up / hold thread to the right—slide
under from outside /

USES
Wide borders.

REMARKS
Very decorative and worked very quickly.

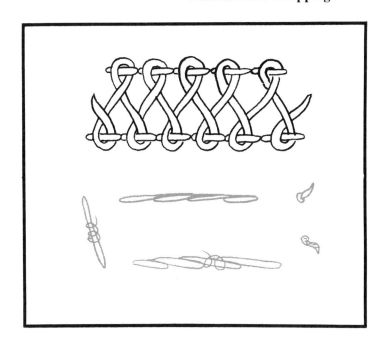

Set foundation of two parallel lines
of Holbein stitch. Stagger second line.
(Back or running stitch may be sub-
stituted.)

D.O.W. →

Step 1.   Bring thread up at A; pull
through. Make a loop up and around
to the right. Slide needle under first
stitch and over loop; pull through
loosely. Do not pierce the fabric.

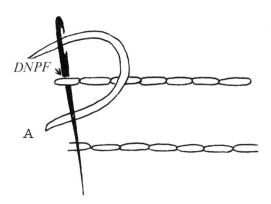

Step 2.   Make a loop down and around
to the right. Slide needle under first
stitch on lower line and, with loop beneath needle, pull through loosely.

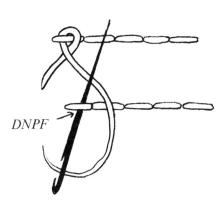

Note

If stitches are not staggered, an
interesting slant develops in the
whipping, particularly useful in
filling in treetrunk designs.

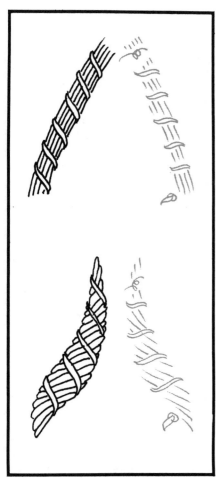

Make a foundation of a bundle of loose threads laid over line to be covered. These threads may be set in as long running stitches, if preferred.

Steps 1 and 2. Lay foundation stitches with thread of contrasting color, bring needle up at A; pull through. Insert needle at B, very close to foundation stitches, bring up at C and pull through. Continue, working D-E, etc. Whipping stitches may be worked closely or spaced, but should cross foundation at almost right angles.

D.O.W. ↗

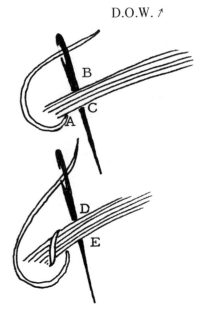

Steps 3 and 4. With a slanted satin stitch foundation, the working method is the same as above. First set in foundation stitches in slanted satin (see B.10).

RHYTHM
(Whipping only) Up / slide under /
USES
Adds interest to border stitches or leaf shape.
REMARKS
Don't overdo it!

RHYTHM
(Whipping only) Up / slide under /
USES
Very decorative wide border, slightly raised.
REMARKS
A hard stitch to keep even, but great effect when finished. Try shading colors.

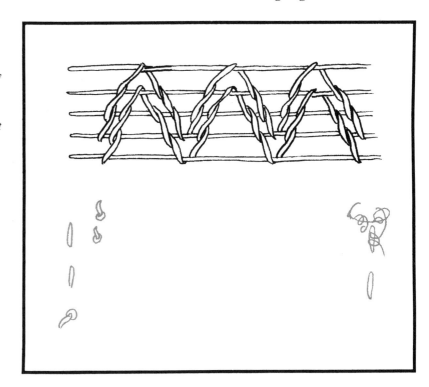

Step 1. Lay foundation of long, straight stitches. Bring thread up at A; pull through. Slide needle down under second straight stitch (do not pierce fabric) and pull through loosely. Continue whipping in this manner until as many stitches as desired are formed.

D.O.W. →

DNPF

A

Step 2. To come down the right side of the triangle, slide the needle up under each straight stitch. Continue until area is filled.

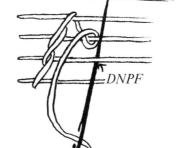

DNPF

Note

Triangles may be completely filled by starting with one stitch instead of three as shown.

family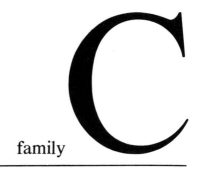

CHAIN STITCHES

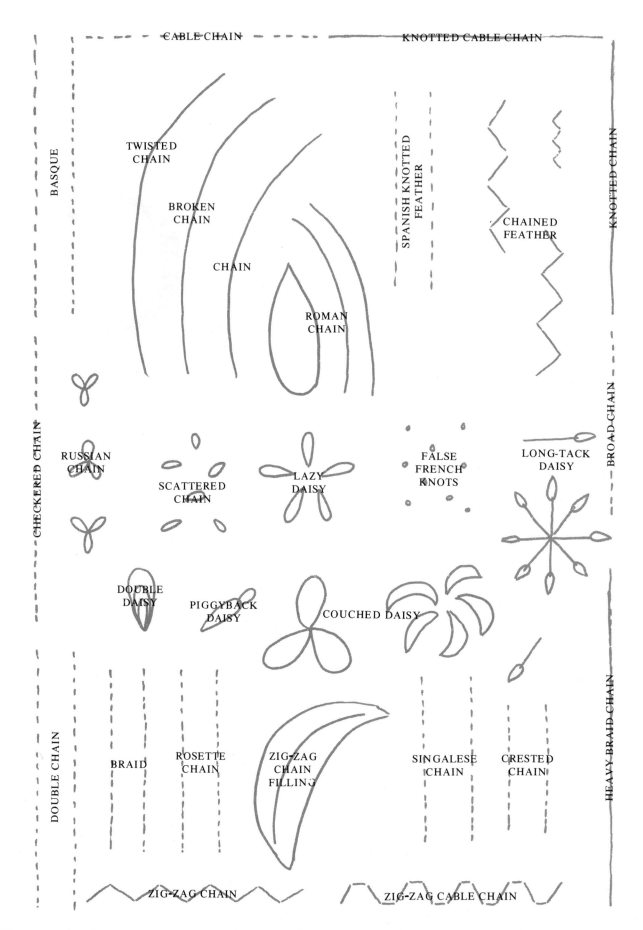

CABLE CHAIN

KNOTTED CABLE CHAIN

BASQUE

KNOTTED CHAIN

TWISTED
CHAIN

BROKEN
CHAIN

CHAIN

ROMAN
CHAIN

SPANISH KNOTTED
FEATHER

CHAINED
FEATHER

CHECKERED CHAIN

BROAD CHAIN

RUSSIAN
CHAIN

SCATTERED
CHAIN

LAZY
DAISY

FALSE
FRENCH
KNOTS

LONG-TACK
DAISY

DOUBLE
DAISY

PIGGYBACK
DAISY

COUCHED DAISY

DOUBLE CHAIN

HEAVY-BRAID CHAIN

BRAID

ROSETTE
CHAIN

ZIG-ZAG
CHAIN
FILLING

SINGALESE
CHAIN

CRESTED
CHAIN

ZIG-ZAG CHAIN

ZIG-ZAG CABLE CHAIN

family C   Chain Stitches

Basic rhythm: up / loop down and around—down—up /

Progression of difficulty

Isolated (Basic Stitch)   1. LAZY DAISY (Detached Chain, Scattered Chain)

Isolated Variations   2. DAISY VARIATIONS: DOUBLE DAISY, PIGGYBACK
  DAISY, COUCHED DAISY, LONG-TACK DAISY

Line   3. CHAIN
  4. BROKEN CHAIN
  5. ROMAN CHAIN (Open Chain)
  6. TWISTED CHAIN
  7. BASQUE (Twisted Daisy Border)
  8. CABLE CHAIN
  9. CHECKERED CHAIN (Magic Chain)
  10. DOUBLE CHAIN (Closed Vertical Feather)
  11. HEAVY BRAID CHAIN (Broad and Reversed Chain)

Angled Line   12. ZIG-ZAG CHAIN AND FILLING
  13. ZIG-ZAG CABLE CHAIN
  14. SPANISH (Twisted Zig-zag Chain, Spanish Knotted Feather)

Grouped   15. RUSSIAN CHAIN

Combined   16. KNOTTED CHAIN
  17. KNOTTED CABLE CHAIN
  18. BRAID
  19. ROSETTE CHAIN
  20. CRESTED CHAIN
  21. CHAINED FEATHER
  22. SINGALESE CHAIN

C.1 LAZY DAISY STITCH
Detached Chain Stitch, Scattered Chain Stitch

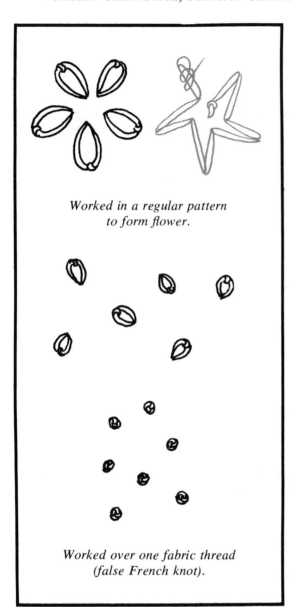

*Worked in a regular pattern
to form flower.*

*Worked over one fabric thread
(false French knot).*

D.O.W. Any

Step 1. Bring thread up at A and pull through. Make a loop in the direction of the other end of the petal. Insert needle into the same hole at A, bring up at B and pull thread up through loop, pulling in the direction the needle points, until loose loop is formed.

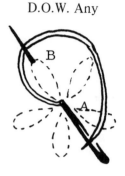

Step 2. Insert needle into same hole at B, but from the outside of the loop to form tack stitch. Bring out at C and pull through.

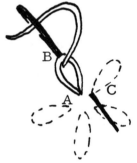

RHYTHM
Up / loop around—down same hole—up other end of loop / tack

USES
Flower petals or centers, leaves, scattered (no pattern), filling.

REMARKS
Two important points! When forming loops, let the thread fall in a natural loop, curving in the direction it wants to go. Insert the needle toward the open side of the loop alongside the first thread, taking care not to split that thread. When working stitch over a printed or stamped design, make point B just short of the line (to the inside of the loop) so that thread will cover the stamped line when pulled up.

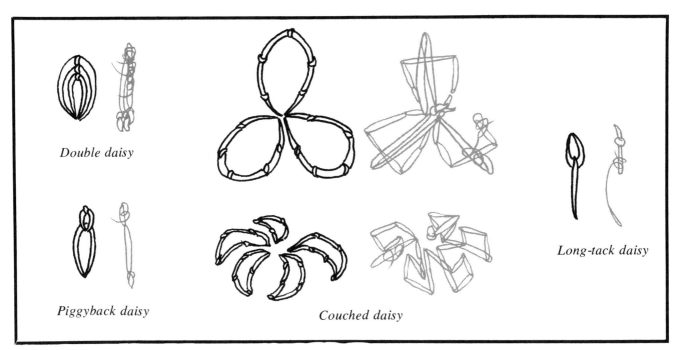

Double daisy

Long-tack daisy

Piggyback daisy

Couched daisy

D.O.W. Any

DOUBLE DAISY STITCH. Work ring of daisy stitches. With another shade of the same color, work a larger daisy around first ones. A third set may then be worked. Do not pull loops up too tightly.

RHYTHM
Up / loop around—down same hole—up through other end of loop / etc.

USES
Flowers, fillings, the ear of a mouse? See B.16.

REMARKS
Sizes and shapes can be as many and varied as your mind can conceive. Play a little!

PIGGYBACK DAISY STITCH. Work long daisy stitch; do not tack. Work short daisy stitch and tack it.

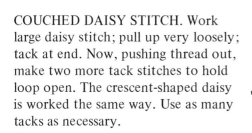

COUCHED DAISY STITCH. Work large daisy stitch; pull up very loosely; tack at end. Now, pushing thread out, make two more tack stitches to hold loop open. The crescent-shaped daisy is worked the same way. Use as many tacks as necessary.

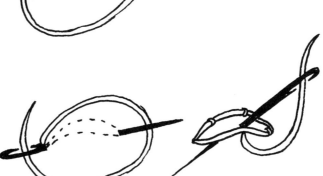

LONG-TACK DAISY STITCH. Work small daisy. Instead of regular tack stitch, make the tack stitch (Ⓣ) about twice as long as the loop. Very nice when arranged in a wheel.

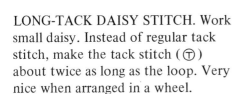

C.3 CHAIN STITCH

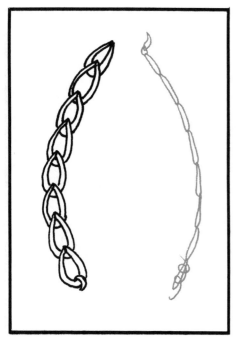

RHYTHM
Up / loop down and around—down same hole—up other end of loop /

USES
Line covering, outlining, branches, stems, etc.

REMARKS
Crewel from India is usually worked entirely in chain stitch. For shading in Jacobean patterns, just work row upon row of chain, following contours. Chain stitch may be whipped or laced to decorate it further (see working method for whipped or laced running stitch, A.17). Both sides of the stitch, or only one side may be whipped—try it!

Step 1. Bring needle up at A; pull through. Make a loop down and around to the right, holding thread with left thumb. Insert needle at A (in same hole) and bring out at B. Pull needle through loop and down towards you. Do not pull loop up too tightly.

Step 2. Make a loop down and around to the right, holding thread down with left thumb. Insert needle at B, inside first loop, making sure needle is in the same hole. Bring out at C; pull through.

Step 3. When line is complete, make a tack stitch to hold last loop down by inserting needle into the same hold (D) but from the outside of the loop. Pull through to the back and knot off.

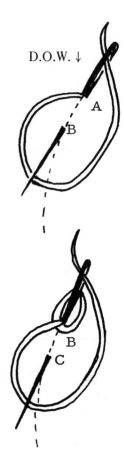

D.O.W. ↓

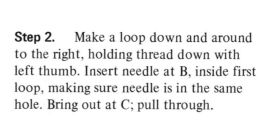

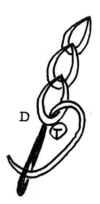

Step 1. Bring thread up at A; pull through. Make a loop, down and around to the right, using left thumb to hold in place. Insert needle at B, bring up at C and pull thread up through loop.

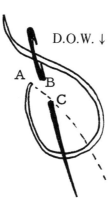

D.O.W. ↓

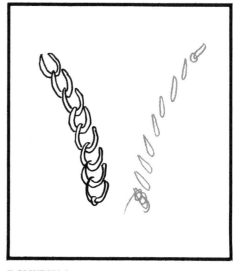

Step 2. Make loop of thread down and around to the right, insert needle at D (just outside first loop and to the right), bring needle up at E and pull through loop. Continue, ending line by tacking last loop down.

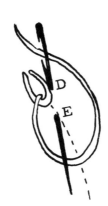

RHYTHM
Up / loop down and around—down same hole—up other end / loop

USES
Shaded lines—twigs, stems, etc.

REMARKS
Because the broken (open) side of this stitch is not solid, it will appear lighter in color. Keep open side on top of the curve to help carry out the illusion of two colors.

C.5 ROMAN CHAIN STITCH
Open Chain

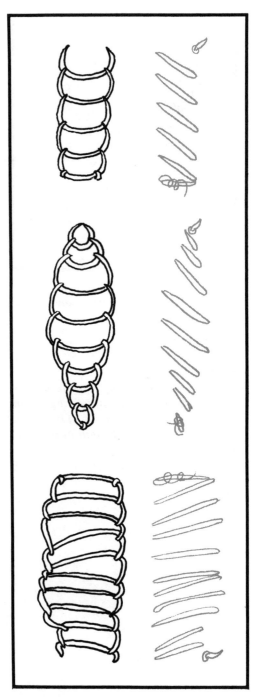

D.O.W. ↓

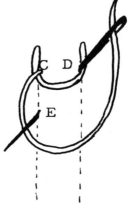

Step 1. Bring thread up at A; pull through. Make loop with thread down and around to the right, holding loop down with thumb. Insert needle at B; bring across diagonally to C, bring up at C and pull up through loop loosely.

Step 2. Make loop down and around to right. With point of needle, drag first loop over to line at D, then insert needle (inside first loop); bring up at E and pull through loosely.

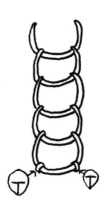

Remember that loops must be loose enough to make a corner at D; allow extra thread. When ending, make two tack stitches (Ⓣ) one at each corner.

RHYTHM
Up / loop down and around—pull over —down—diagonally across—up /

USES
Wide lines.

REMARKS
This stitch is particularly interesting when varied in height and width. Increasing size of loop may be done quickly, but decreasing must be done gradually or loops have a tendency to "fall in." If a little "leg" shows on the outside of a loop, you are not allowing enough extra thread in your loop; slack up on the tension.

D.O.W. ↙

Step 1. Bring thread up at A and pull through. Make a loop down and around to the right. Insert needle at B and bring out at C, making a slanting stitch back to the line. Pull through loop.

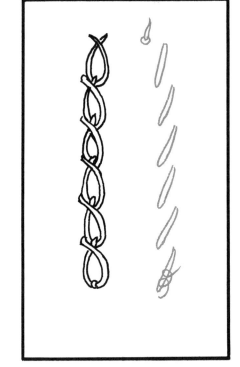

Step 2. Make loop down and around to the right. Insert needle at D, just outside loop formed in Step 1. Pull through loop.

Step 3. Continue in this manner until end of the line. Stitches should be worked closely together but should be pulled up loosely to maintain the correct effect. End with tack stitch (Ⓣ).

RHYTHM
Up / loop down and around to right —down—up inside base of loop /

USES
Slightly raised lines. When used row upon row as a filling stitch, an interesting texture is produced.

REMARKS
This stitch is very much like the coral stitch. The length of the stitch is the difference.

C.7 BASQUE STITCH
Twisted Daisy Border Stitch

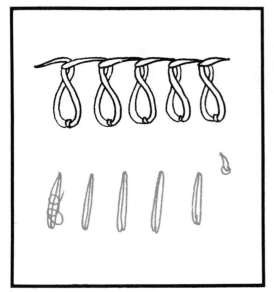

RHYTHM
Up / down—up—twist loop around needle /
down for tack—up at top /

USES
Wide borders.

REMARKS
Try various lengths of stitch on this one; it is
great for decorative borders.

D.O.W. →

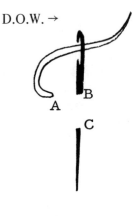

Step 1. Bring thread up at A; pull
through. Insert needle at B bring up at
C; do not pull through.

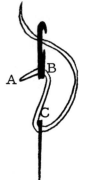

Step 2. Wrap thread around needle
as shown. Thread should be snug. Now
pull needle through.

Step 3. Tack daisy down, insert
needle at C (outside loop) and bring
up again at B; pull through. Place second stitch at D and E. Continue to
end of line. Finish by tacking top
corner to hold in place.

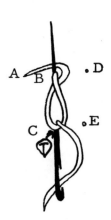

Step 1. Bring thread up at A and pull through. Lay work on lap. Hold needle in right hand, grasp thread in left and wrap thread once around needle as shown.

D.O.W. ←

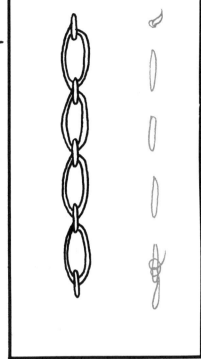

Step 2. Still holding thread in left hand, snug around needle, insert point at B, bring out at C, and bring thread under point of needle. Pull snug. Now pull needle and thread through.

Step 3. Continue until end of line. End stitch by making a long tack stitch, pulling thread to the back and knotting off.

RHYTHM
Up / needle under—wrap thread around—down—up—snug thread under point /

USES
Medium-width borders.

REMARKS
Looks like a heavy linked chain.

Note

Spacing of stitches is important. Make spaces from C to B a little longer than spaces from B to A. Work very evenly for best effect.

C.9 CHECKERED CHAIN STITCH
Magic Chain Stitch

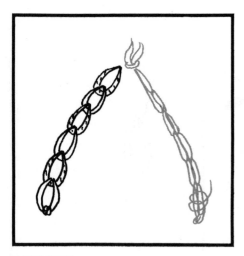

RHYTHM
Up / hold light thread to side—loop down and around with dark. Down in same hole—up at base of loop / hold dark thread to the side, etc.

USES
Very decorative line stitch, "conversation" stitch.

REMARKS
Tension must be kept even on both threads at all times.

Thread two contrasting colors through the needle; knot one end and make sure the tension is equal on both threads.

Step 1.   Bring needle up at A, pull through. Separate the two threads; make a loop down and around to the right with first thread and hold the second off to the right side. Insert needle again at A bring up at B, and, with loop beneath the needle, pull through loop.

Step 2.   Make sure second color is pulled all the way through (tension will be uneven). Holding first color off to the right, make a loop down and around to the right. Insert again at B (inside loop in the same hole with threads), bring up at C and pull through loop. Tension will be even again. Continue until line is covered. After completing the last "pair" (tension even), tack last loop down. Both threads will show on tack stitch.

D.O.W. ↓

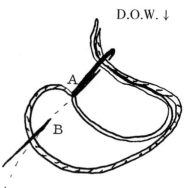

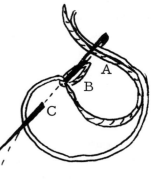

D.O.W. ↓

Step 1.   Bring thread up at A; pull through. Make loop down and around to right. Insert needle at B, bring up at C with thread beneath needle and pull through.

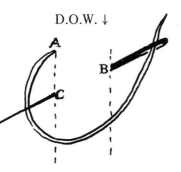

Step 2.   Make loop down and around to right. Insert needle again at B; bring up at D with thread beneath needle and pull through.

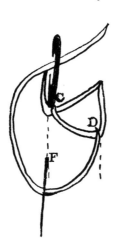

Step 3.   Make loop down and around to left. Insert needle again at C, bring up at E, and, with loop beneath needle, pull through. Continue. Making a loop to the left, work on paralled lines. To finish, tack last loop down.

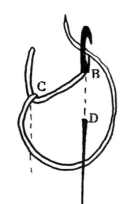

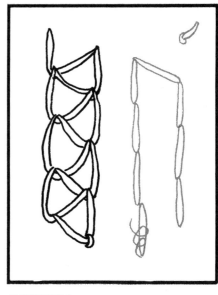

RHYTHM
Up / loop to the right, down—up through loop, loop to the left—down —up through loop / (A typical feather rhythm.)

USES
A wide border stitch, quickly worked.

REMARKS
Keep in mind little triangles, their bases alternating on the outside lines. When you work the open vertical feather, you will notice the only difference in these two stitches is that this one goes down into the loop previously formed, whereas open vertical feather does not.

C.11 HEAVY BRAID CHAIN STITCH
Broad or Reversed Chain Stitch

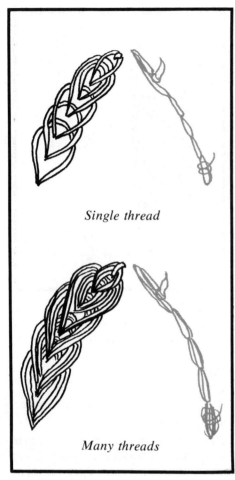

Single thread

Many threads

RHYTHM
(After first daisy) Up / slide through stitch above—down same hole /

USES
Wide border stitch; heavy chain gives raised effect.

REMARKS
Color combinations are interesting in this stitch for they do not always stay in the same order each time.

Thread 3 or more contrasting colors through large needle.

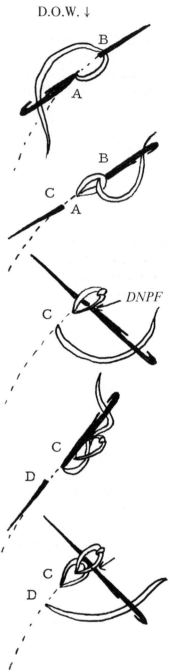

D.O.W. ↓

Step 1.   Bring threads up at A; pull through. Insert needle again at A; make loop up and around to left. Bring needle up at B and pull up through loop.

Step 2.   Make tack stitch by inserting needle (outside loop) again in B and bring up at C; pull through.

Step 3.   Slide needle under first chain. Do not pierce fabric.

DNPF

Step 4.   Insert needle again at C; bring up at D, pull through.

Step 5.   Again slide needle through first chain; pull through and insert again at D. Continue, always sliding needle under second stitch above (not the one just completed). Do not pull loops tightly; a loose loop gives a very full, rich effect. Lifting up loop with needle when sliding helps to maintain even tension on all threads.

Note

Steps 1 through 4 produce a broad chain. The stitch may be continued in this manner, sliding subsequent stitches through the one directly above. However, sliding the next stitch through the one two loops back will produce the heavy braid chain.

RHYTHM
Up / (zig) make loop—down same hole—up inside loop / (zag) make loop—down—up at right angle inside loop /

USES
Wide borders; row upon row makes a wonderful filling stitch, perhaps for a leaf.

REMARKS
Be careful of the angles; more than a right angle is acceptable but less and the stitch will slide down on itself and look sloppy!

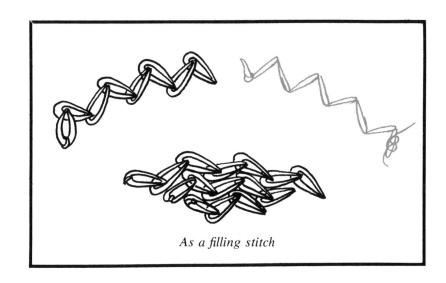

As a filling stitch

Step 1. Bring thread up at A; pull through. Make a loop up and around to the right and hold it in place with left thumb. Insert needle again at A the same hole (A); bring up at B, slanting stitch diagonally across line. Loop formed should be longer than a regular chain stitch. Pull thread up through loop.

D.O.W.

Step 2. Make a loop down and around to the right and hold it in place with left thumb. Insert needle in same hole (B) with working thread and bring up at C; pull thread up through loop. Note that stitches form a right angle.

Step 3. Make a loop up and around to the right; insert needle again at C (inside loop) and bring up at D; pull thread up through loop. This stitch will match the direction of the first stitch.

Note

For filling work one row next to another very closely. Change shading as you go along.

C.13 ZIG-ZAG CABLE CHAIN STITCH

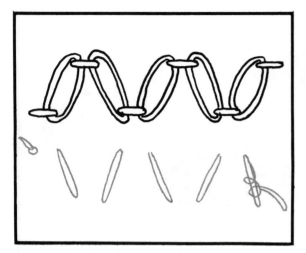

RHYTHM
Up / wrap around—down—up—loop around /
USES
*Wide border stitch; worked evenly, row upon row,
makes a fascinating filling.*

REMARKS
*Be sure wrapping is snug before pulling through.
Easier if you learn the cable chain first.*

Step 1. Bring thread up at A; pull through. Wrap thread once around needle, holding thread tight, insert at B, and bring loop under needle at C. Pull thread snug before pulling through fabric.

D.O.W. ←

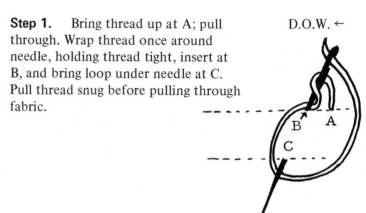

Step 2. Wrap thread around needle; still holding thread in left hand, insert needle at D and bring out at E. (E-D is at right angle with B-C). Bring thread under needle at E and pull snug. Now pull thread through.

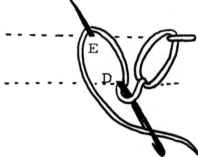

Twisted Zig-zag Chain Stitch, Spanish Knotted Feather Stitch

Work coral stitch (G.7) before you do this one.

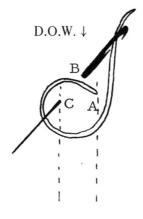

D.O.W. ↓

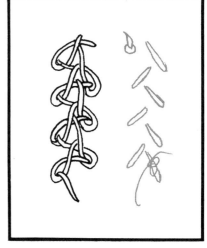

Step 1. Bring thread up at A; pull through. Make loop up and around to the left and down around to the right. Insert needle at B (outside loop) and bring up at C (inside loop) and, thread beneath needle, pull through.

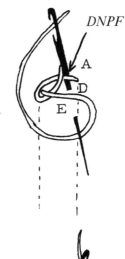

DNPF

Step 2. Slide needle under stitch just to left of A. Do not pierce fabric. Insert needle at D, bring up at E and make a loop under needle from left to right. Pull through.

RHYTHM
Up / loop—down—up / down in center—up—twist loop around /

USES
Very decorative borders.

REMARKS
This stitch is difficult to keep even. Practice will help!

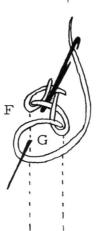

Step 3. Slide needle under lower part of square formed between first two stitches; insert needle just below at F and bring out at G. (The new loop repeats Step 1.) With loop beneath needle, pull through.

Note

Loops may be made before needle is inserted and held in place with left thumb. If you prefer, loops (especially Step 2) may be wound around the needle when it is in position.

C.15 RUSSIAN CHAIN STITCH

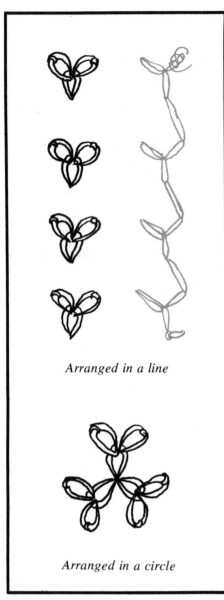

Arranged in a line

Arranged in a circle

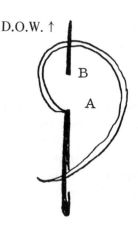

Step 1. Bring thread up at A; pull through. Make loop up and around insert needle at A, bring up at B (loop beneath needle) and pull through.

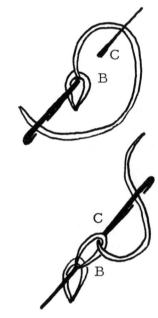

Step 2. Make loop up and around, insert needle again at B bring up at C (loop beneath needle) and pull through.

Step 3. Make tack stitch by inserting needle at C (outside loop); bring up at B and pull through.

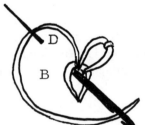

Step 4. Make loop up and around to left, insert needle again at B, bring up at D (loop beneath needle) and pull through. Make a tack stitch at D to finish.

RHYTHM
Up / loop around—down same hole—up end of loop / (repeat three times)

USES
Decorative isolated or as a border or line of stitches. Forms a flower shape when worked in a circle.

REMARKS
Try combining with French knots, Italian knots, etc.

D.O.W. ←

Step I. Bring thread up at A; pull through. Insert needle at B and bring up at C; pull through.

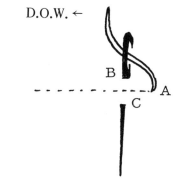

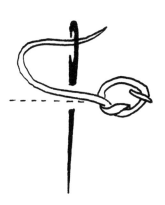

Step 2. Holding loop of thread up and around to the right, slide needle under stitch (B-A) from top to bottom. Do not pierce fabric. Pull through loosely until small circle is formed.

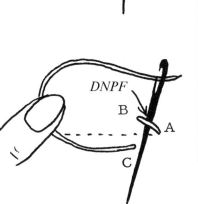

RHYTHM
Up / down—up / slide under, loop around, slide through loop /
USES
Wide borders or lines.
REMARKS
Make all the adjustments on size of loop before pulling through. Works best with heavy yarn.

Step 3. Still holding small circle down with thumb, slide needle under loop at top, over loop at bottom and over working thread. Continue to pull in the direction needle is pointing.

Step 4. Repeat Step 1. Continue to end of line; finish with a long tack stitch.

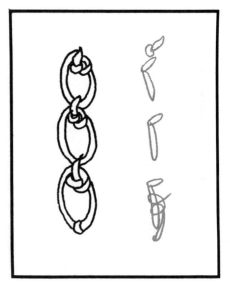

RHYTHM

Up / loop around—down—up through loop / slide under—loop around—down (outside)—up—inside loop /

USES

Wide border stitch.

REMARKS

It will be easier if you are familiar with the coral stitch (see G.7) before attempting this one.

Step 1.   Bring thread up at A; pull through. Holding thread above the line to the left, make loop down and around to right. Insert needle at B (outside loop) and bring up at C so that loop is beneath needle. Pull through.

Step 2.   Slide needle under thread next to A, from bottom to top. Do not pierce fabric. Pull through.

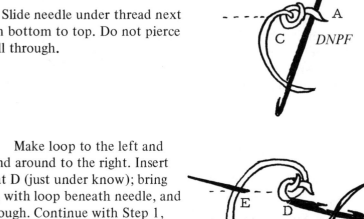

Step 3.   Make loop to the left and down and around to the right. Insert needle at D (just under know); bring up at E, with loop beneath needle, and pull through. Continue with Step 1, etc. To finish, make a tack stitch over final loop.

Step 1.   Bring thread up at A; pull through. Twist a loop in the thread as shown.

D.O.W. ←

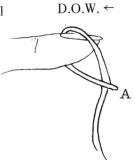

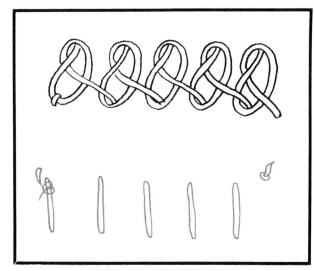

Step 2.   Insert needle inside twisted loop at B; bring needle up at C and pass thread under point of needle. Adjust stitch before pulling through. Continue with Steps 1 and 2 to cover area. Tack last stitch to finish off.

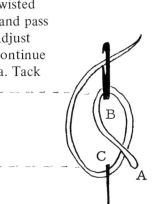

RHYTHM
Up / twist loop—down in loop—up—snug thread under needle /

USES
Very wide border stitch.

REMARKS
Tension is the most important part of this stitch; it takes practice to work evenly!

Note

This stitch should be worked close together and small or it will not stay in place. Experimenting with size and weight of thread will help to judge proper placement.

C.19 ROSETTE CHAIN STITCH

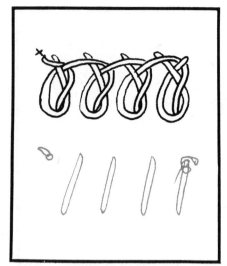

RHYTHM
Up / down—up—twist / slide /
USES
Wide borders.
REMARKS
Do not pull the loops up too tightly or "legs" will appear on top, spoiling the effect of the stitch.

Step 1. Bring thread up at A; pull through. Make loop down and around to the right and hold loop down with left thumb. Insert needle at B; bring out at C so that loop is beneath needle and pull through.

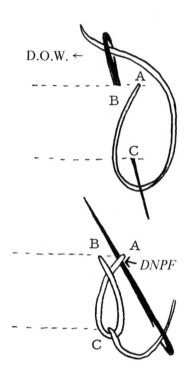

Step 2. Slide needle under stitch near A, from bottom to top. Do not pierce fabric. Hold loop down with thumb while pulling thread up through material.

Step 3. Make loop down and around to right and hold in place with left thumb. Insert at D; bring up at E so that loop is beneath needle; pull through.

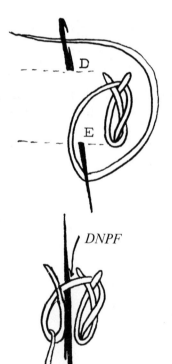

Step 4. Holding loop down with left thumb, slide needle under thread without piercing fabric. Continue to end; insert needle just to the left of the last stitch (marked X on finished diagram).

D.O.W. ↓

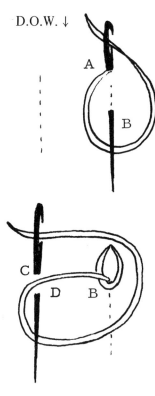

Step 1. Bring thread up at A; pull through. Make loop down and around to the right, insert needle again at A, bring out at B so that loop is beneath needle and pull through.

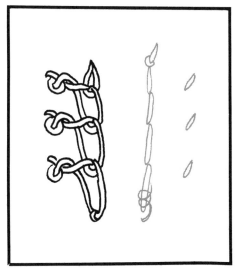

Step 2. Make wide loop to left, curving down and around to the right. Hold down with thumb. Insert needle at C (outside of loop) and bring up at D (inside loop). Pull through. (G-D is directly across from B).

RHYTHM
Up / down same hole—loop around—up / "C" loop—down—up—tiny slant / slide /

USES
Wide border stitch; work around outside of a circle for flowers.

REMARKS
This stitch combines the chain and the coral stitch and is easier if both basic stitches are familiar before you start this one.

DNPF

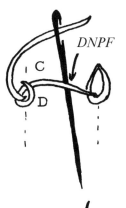

Step 3. Slide needle under center thread, from top to bottom. Do not pierce fabric. Pull through gently.

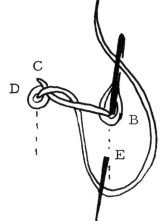

Step 4. Make loop down and around to the right; insert needle again at B (inside first chain). Bring up at E, over loop, and pull through. To finish, tack-stitch last loop.

C.21 CHAINED FEATHER STITCH

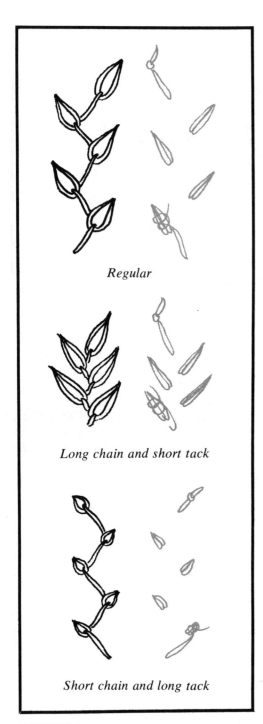

Regular

Long chain and short tack

Short chain and long tack

D.O.W. ↓

Step 1. Bring thread up at A; pull through. Make a loop down and around to the right. Insert needle in same hole at A; bring up at B (loop beneath needle) and pull through loosely.

Step 2. Insert needle at C and bring up at D; pull through.

Step 3. Make a loop down and around to the left; insert needle again at D; bring up at C (loop beneath needle) and pull through.

Step 4. Insert at E, bring up at F, etc. Variations are diagrammed at the right.

RHYTHM
Up / loop around—down—up base of loop / down (long tack)—up /

USES
Wide borders, lifelike branches with buds, or stems with flowers.

REMARKS
Although this stitch is called a feather, the working method is that of the chains. Don't let the name confuse you on the rhythm!

D.O.W. ↓

B   A

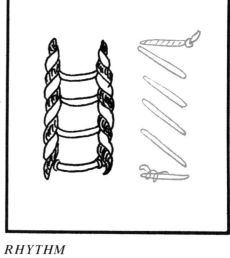

Step 1.   With thread of contrasting color
(1) twice as long as area to be covered,
insert needle at A and bring up at B. Pull
halfway through so that two long loose
threads cover dotted lines. Do not attach
other ends.

C D

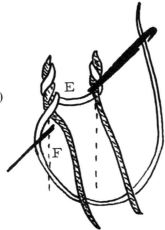

E

Step 2.   With color 2 in needle, bring
thread up at C and pull through. Make loop
down and around to right. Insert needle at
D and bring out at E (loop beneath needle)
and pull through, bringing 1 threads up the
loop before pulling loop completely closed.

RHYTHM
Up / loop around—twist other thread
—down—diagonally across—up /

USES
Wide decorative borders.

REMARKS
Almost the same effect is created by
working Roman chain (see C.5) and then
whipping each side. The twist of the
threads is slightly different.

E

Step 3.   Twist left thread 1 around 2.
Make loop down and around to right; pull
both 1 threads up through loop. Insert
needle at E (push first loop over with point)
and bring out at F so that new loop is beneath needle. Pull through. To finish, tack
stitch both corners of last loop and bring
ends of 1 threads to back and knot off.

F

family **D**

BUTTONHOLE OR BLANKET STITCHES

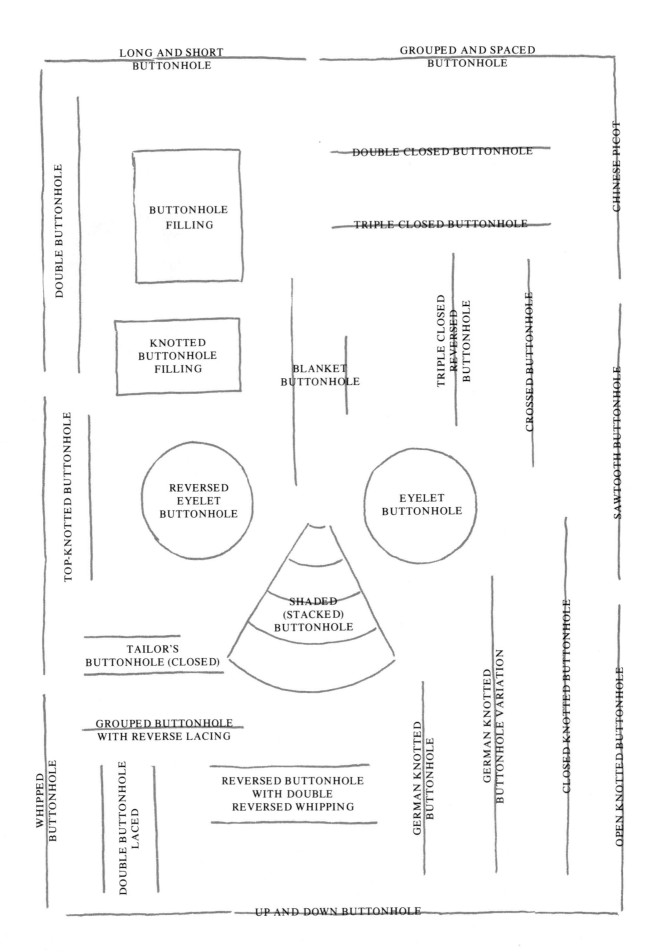

LONG AND SHORT
BUTTONHOLE

GROUPED AND SPACED
BUTTONHOLE

DOUBLE BUTTONHOLE

CHINESE PICOT

DOUBLE CLOSED BUTTONHOLE

BUTTONHOLE
FILLING

TRIPLE CLOSED BUTTONHOLE

KNOTTED
BUTTONHOLE
FILLING

TRIPLE CLOSED
REVERSED
BUTTONHOLE

CROSSED BUTTONHOLE

BLANKET
BUTTONHOLE

TOP-KNOTTED BUTTONHOLE

SAWTOOTH BUTTONHOLE

REVERSED
EYELET
BUTTONHOLE

EYELET
BUTTONHOLE

SHADED
(STACKED)
BUTTONHOLE

TAILOR'S
BUTTONHOLE (CLOSED)

CLOSED KNOTTED BUTTONHOLE

OPEN KNOTTED BUTTONHOLE

GROUPED BUTTONHOLE
WITH REVERSE LACING

WHIPPED
BUTTONHOLE

DOUBLE BUTTONHOLE
LACED

REVERSED BUTTONHOLE
WITH DOUBLE
REVERSED WHIPPING

GERMAN KNOTTED
BUTTONHOLE

GERMAN KNOTTED
BUTTONHOLE VARIATION

UP AND DOWN BUTTONHOLE

family D   Buttonhole or Blanket Stitches

Basic rhythm: up / loop down and around—down—up /

Progression of difficulty

Line (Basic Stitch)   1. BUTTONHOLE (Blanket)
2. BUTTONHOLE VARIATIONS: DOUBLE BUTTONHOLE, LONG AND SHORT BUTTONHOLE, GROUPED AND SPACED BUTTONHOLE, CHINESE PICOT BUTTONHOLE, SAWTOOTH BUTTONHOLE

Angled   3. CLOSED BUTTONHOLE AND VARIATIONS: DOUBLE CLOSED BUTTONHOLE, TRIPLE CLOSED BUTTONHOLE, TRIPLE REVERSED BUTTONHOLE, CROSSED BUTTONHOLE

Stacked   4. SHADED BUTTONHOLE FILLING (Overlapping or Stacked Buttonhole)

Grouped   5. EYELET BUTTONHOLE, REVERSED EYELET BUTTONHOLE

Combined   6. TOP-KNOTTED BUTTONHOLE
7. KNOTTED BUTTONHOLE
8. GERMAN KNOTTED BUTTONHOLE
9. TAILOR'S BUTTONHOLE
10. UP AND DOWN BUTTONHOLE
11. LACED BUTTONHOLE VARIATIONS: DOUBLE LACED, GROUPED REVERSE LACING, REVERSED BUTTONHOLE WITH DOUBLE REVERSED WHIPPING
12. BUTTONHOLE FILLING
13. KNOTTED BUTTONHOLE FILLING

D.1 BUTTONHOLE STITCH
Blanket Stitch

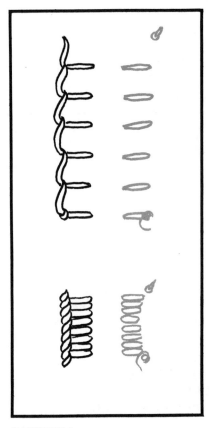

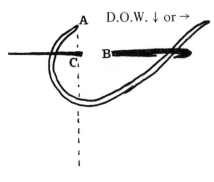

Step 1.   Bring thread up at A; pull through. Make a loop to the left of the line and down and around to the right. Insert needle at B; bring out at C (just inside of line to be covered). With loop beneath needle, pull through.

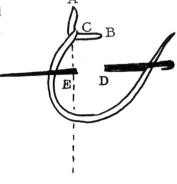

Step 2.   Make a loop down and around to the right. Insert needle at D and bring out at E. With loop beneath needle, pull through. Notice that C and E do not come quite to the line to be covered.

RHYTHM

Up / form a loop with left thumb—down—perpendicularly back to line—down—up / loop under needle

USES

Worked closely, as a finishing edge on a blanket (hence the name) or around a line to be slit later, such as a buttonhole. Use in medium to broad width to applique one fabric on another.

REMARKS

When pulling thread through, catch thread with left thumb so next loop will be all ready. Do not bring point of needle quite to the printed line so that completed stitch will cover line. Remember, working thread is always on line for buttonholes.

Step 3.   Continue to end of line. Make a tack stitch over last loop to hold it down. Tack stitch: insert needle in same hole where working thread is coming up, but from the outisde of the loop.

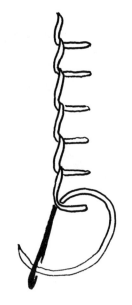

Note

Closed buttonhole is worked in the same manner but stitches are placed so closely that no fabric shows between.

RHYTHM
Up / loop—down—up through loop /

USES
Curved slanting lines such as hills and ground areas, around circular flowers, or double on sides of heavy stems, leaves, stalks; picot and sawtooth work very well on edges, giving a firm, double-sided finish.

REMARKS
These are only a few variations; many more combinations may be arranged.

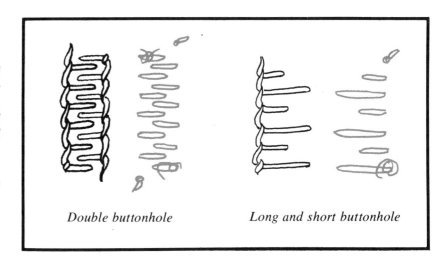

Double buttonhole   *Long and short buttonhole*

Note

These are only a few of the possible combinations for achieving variations in the buttonhole stitch. The working method is the same as regular buttonhole or blanket stitch.

D.O.W. ↓ or →

Slanted long and short buttonhole

Grouped and spaced buttonhole

Chinese picot buttonhole

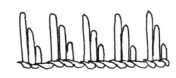

Sawtooth buttonhole

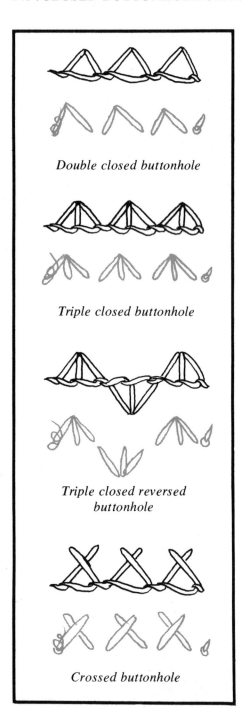

Double closed buttonhole

Triple closed buttonhole

Triple closed reversed buttonhole

Crossed buttonhole

D.O.W. →

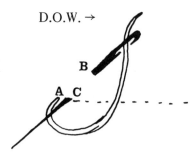

Step 1.   Bring thread up at A; pull through. Make a loop down and around to the right. Insert needle at B, bring out at C with loop beneath needle; pull through.

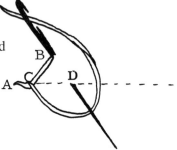

Step 2.   Make a loop down and around to the right. Insert needle again at B, bring out at D with loop beneath needle; pull through.

Note

The working methods are the same for the variations of closed buttonhole stitch diagrammed on the left. Remember that the working thread is always on the line to be covered.

RHYTHM
Up / loop around—down—up / pull to form corner

USES
As an edging. As a wide line good for stems, branches, etc.

REMARKS
Many other variations are possible. Try working these as tiny stitches to finish off an eyeglass case, etc.

RHYTHM
Up / loop around—down—up /

USES
To fill an area, such as a flower petal, a circle or a hill. Very nice in a fan-shaped arc or circular area.

REMARKS
In shading, it usually looks better if the darkest shades are used first in the smallest arc and each subsequent line is worked in a lighter shade to the outside. Hills appear rounder if bottoms or lower parts are worked in darker shades and top edges in lightest with intermediate shades in between.

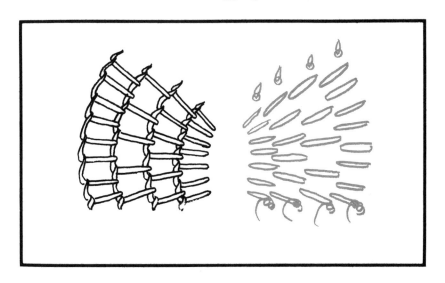

For working method see eyelet buttonhole (D.5).

D.O.W. ↙ Many Journeys

Step 1. Set in first row of buttonhole stitch in darkest shade, work stitches closely.

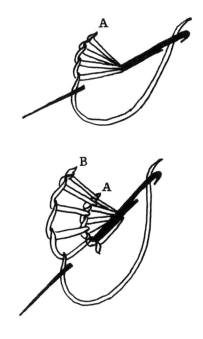

Step 2. Work second row in lighter shade (starting at B). Insert needle inside the stitch formed on the previous row.

Step 3. Work each subsequent row (starting at C,D, etc.) in lighter shades until area is filled. If a more solid filling is desired, two or more stitches may be worked into one space: see last row of diagram on the right. End each row with a tack stitch.

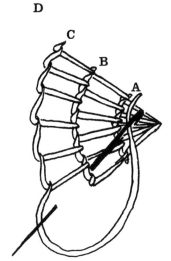

87

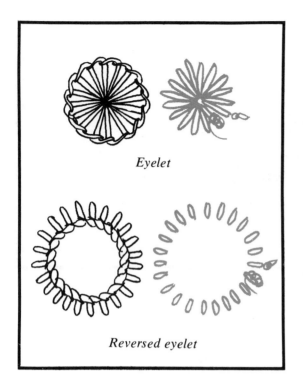

Eyelet

Reversed eyelet

RHYTHM
Up / loop around—down—up /
USES
As a flower or a flower center.
REMARKS
Eyelets were originally used for tiny round buttonholes or on belts, the centers cut out to make a hole. This same technique is interesting in embroidery. The hole may be left open, or an interesting patch sewn on the wrong side so that a contrasting color shows through. Of course, the center does not have to be cut away; try filling it with French knots, for example.

D.O.W. Any

Step 1.   Bring thread up at A; pull through. Make a loop, down and around to the right. Insert needle at B, bring up at C with loop beneath needle; pull through.

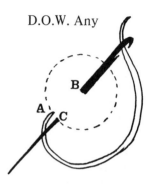

Step 2.   Make a loop down and around to the right. Insert needle again at B (same hole all the way around) bring up at D and pull through. Continue until circle is filled; end with tack stitch.

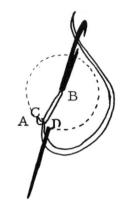

REVERSED EYELET BUTTONHOLE

Same as above but work on the outside of the circle.

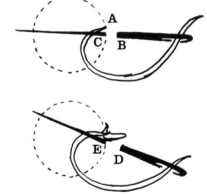

D.O.W. → or ↓

Step 1. Bring thread up at A; pull through. Wrap thread around thumb as shown. Slide needle under loop from bottom to top.

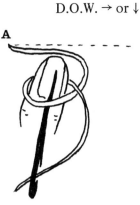

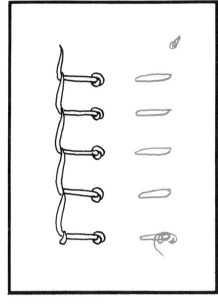

Step 2. Keeping point of needle inside of loop, insert needle at B and bring up at C. Bring needle over thread between A and thumb. (Do not pull through).

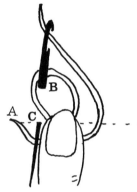

RHYTHM
Up / loop around thumb—needle through loop into fabric (down)—up outside base of loop—tighten /

USES
As a medium to wide line stitch, or work in a circle to make a flower, etc.

REMARKS
The secret of making this stitch is to tighten well before pulling through, and the pull must be down toward you.

Step 3. Tighten loop firmly around by pulling down on thread at arrow. Now pull needle through. Continue to end of line; end with a tack stitch.

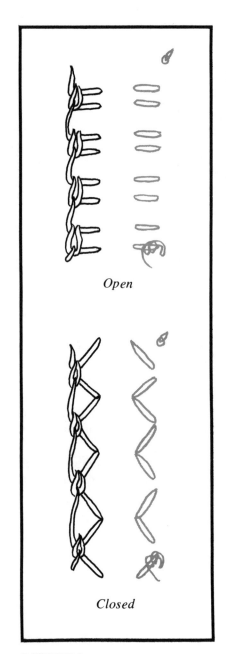

Open

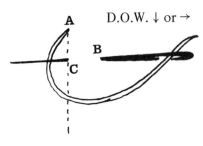

Step 1. Bring thread up at A; pull through. Make a loop, down and around to the right. Insert needle at B, bring up at C (loop under needle) and pull through.

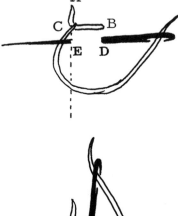

Step 2. Repeat Step 1, spacing stitches as shown.

Step 3. Make a loop down and around to the right. Slide needle under first two stitches (do not pierce fabric). Make sure loop is beneath needle, and pull through. Do not pull loop up too tightly. Continue to end of line, finishing with tack stitch.

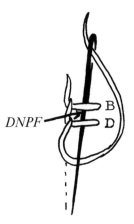

Closed

Note

Working method is the same for closed knotted buttonhole except that stitches are put in at a slant and points B and D are in the same hole.

RHYTHM
Up / loop—down—up / loop —down—up / loop down—slide needle—pull down

USES
Medium wide lines and borders; works well in combination with other stitches.

REMARKS
Don't pull loops too tightly, so that stitches will curve gently.

D.O.W. ↓

Step 1. Bring thread up at A; pull through. Make a loop down and around to the right. Insert needle at B and bring out at C (loop beneath needle); pull through.

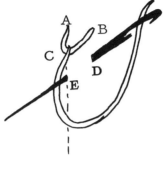

Step 2. Make a loop down and around to the right. Insert needle at D bring out at E and (loop beneath needle) pull through.

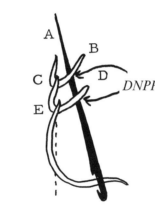

Step 3. Slide needle under both stitches as shown. Do not pierce fabric.

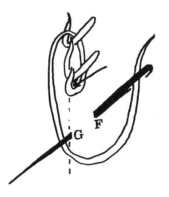

Step 4. Continue, spacing stitches in groups of two. End with a long tack stitch over last group.

Variation

RHYTHM
Up / loop—down—up / loop—down—up / slide needle up under stitches / loop around—down—up / etc.

USES
Medium to wide, very decorative stitch for borders, etc.

REMARKS
Pull last loop very loosely to keep effect.

Note

A pretty variation is made by slipping the needle down through the lowest loop (at arrow) and pulling the knot thus formed a little tighter. See variation.

D.9 TAILOR'S BUTTONHOLE STITCH

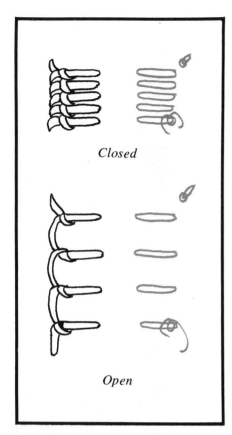

Closed

Open

Step 1. Bring thread up at A; pull through. Wrap thread around thumb as shown. Slide needle under loop from bottom to top.

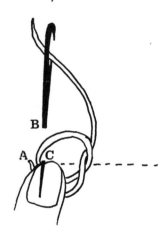

Step 2. Holding loop in place with thumb, pull thread through but leave loop open.

Step 3. Still holding loop in place, insert needle at B (outside loop) and bring up at C (inside loop on line). Do not pull through.

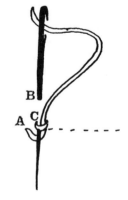

Step 4. Pull working thread to the right to tighten loop around needle. Pull through.

RHYTHM
Up / loop—slide needle through loop—pull up, leaving circle (open knot) down—up inside circle—tighten /

USES
When used by tailors on coats, etc, extra knot gives extra wear. In embroidery, a fancier edge is achieved.

REMARKS
Hardly worth the trouble.

D.O.W. →

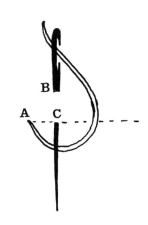

Step 1. Bring thread up at A; pull through. Make a loop down and around to the right. Insert needle at B, bring up at C (loop beneath needle) and pull through.

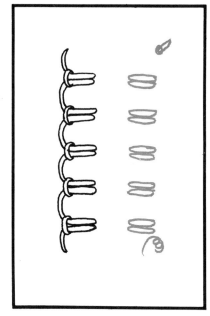

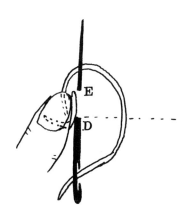

Step 2. Holding first stitch in place with left thumb, make a loop up and around to the right. Insert needle at D, bring up at E (loop beneath needle) and pull through loosely.

RHYTHM
Up / loop down—needle down—up / loop up—needle down—up / (pull up then down)

USES
Decorative edge, medium to wide border.

REMARKS
A very easy stitch to work which looks as if it were difficult.

Step 3. Pull down on working thread until loop formed at C-D is tightened.

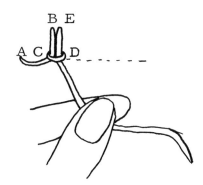

D.11 LACED BUTTONHOLE VARIATIONS

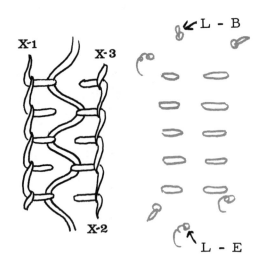

Double buttonhole, laced

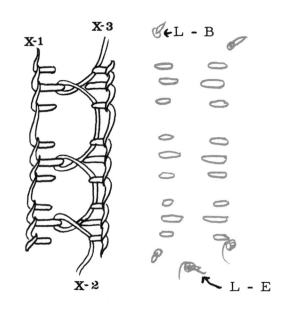

Grouped buttonhole with reverse lacing

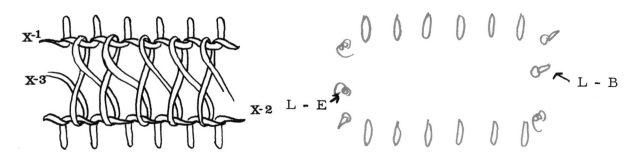

Reversed buttonhole with double reversed whipping

D.O.W. ↓ or →

LB = lacing begins
LE = lacing ends

   Note
The back of the foundation stitches appear on the back of the material. The only parts of the lacing that will show on the back are the knots at the beginning and end.

x = start of each journey

1, 2, 3, = order of work

   Note

Lacing thread pierces fabric *only* at the beginning and end of line.

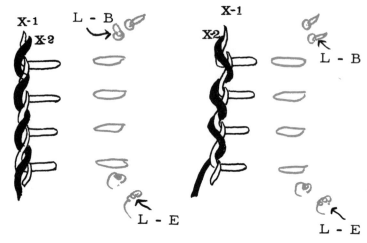

Whipped left to right   Whipped right to left

D.O.W. ⇄ Many Journeys

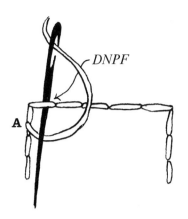

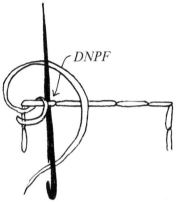

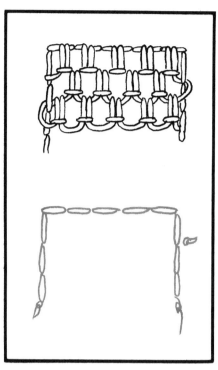

Step 1.   Lay foundation of back (or Holbein) stitches around area to be covered. Bring the thread up at A; pull through. Make a loop, down and around to the right. Slide needle under first foundation stitch, over loop, and pull through loosely. Do not pierce fabric.

Step 2.   Make a loop up and around to the right and slide needle under first foundation stitch (but from below this time); pull thread through with a downward motion. Continue placing two stitches, which do not pierce the fabric, in each of the foundation stitches. Slide needle under foundation stitch at side edge.

Step 3.   Work back in the same manner, but sliding the needle under the loop formed on the previous row.

RHYTHM
Up / loop down—pull (down) through —loop up—pull (up) through—pull down

USES
As filling, works best on a squared area, but may be used in circles.

REMARKS
Only the knots at the beginning and end of the buttonhole filling will show on the back, along with the foundation stitches. The filling "floats."

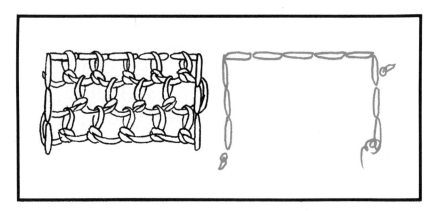

RHYTHM
Up / loop (down) pull through—loop down to form knot

USES
A most decorative filling stitch for any area.

REMARKS
Note that filling "floats." Last line should be tacked. Only foundation stitches show on the back. The filling shows only as beginning and ending knots.

D.O.W. ⇄

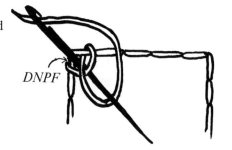

Step 1. Lay foundation of back (or Holbein) stitches around area to be covered. Bring thread up at A; pull through. (Thread may be slipped under top vertical stitch, if preferred.) Make a loop, down and around to the right. Slide needle under first horizontal stitch, over loop, and pull through loosely. Do not pierce fabric.

Step 2. Make a loop down and around to the right. Slide needle under both threads of first loop, then over second loop, and pull through, thus forming a knot. Continue with these two steps to end of row. Slide needle under the top vertical stitch and under the second vertical stitch.

Step 3. Work second row in the same manner, but from right to left. Note slight change in position of threads. Continue until area is covered. Insert needle under last foundation stitch; pull through to back and knot off.

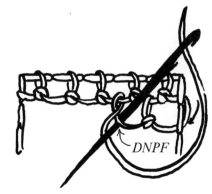

family E

FLY OR FEATHER STITCHES

SINGLE FEATHER

SINGLE FEATHER

FEATHER STITCH

DOUBLE FEATHER

LONG-ARMED FEATHER

FAGGOTING STITCH

FAGGOT FILLING

Y-STITCH FILLING

FLY

CLOSE-STACKED FLY

OPEN VERTICAL FEATHER

CLOSED VERTICAL FEATHER

CLOSED CRETAN

OPEN CRETAN

CLOSE-STACKED FLY

Y-STITCH BORDER

family E   Fly or Feather Stitches

Basic rhythm: up / loop right—down—up / loop left—down—up /

Progression of difficulty

Isolated (Basic Stitch)   1. FLY STITCH, Y-STITCH BORDER AND FILLING

Line   2. SINGLE FEATHER (Slanted Buttonhole)
3. FEATHER
4. DOUBLE FEATHER
5. OPEN VERTICAL FEATHER
6. FAGGOTTING AND FAGGOT FILLING (Straight Open Cretan)

Stacked   7. LONG-ARMED FEATHER (Stacked Feather)
8. CLOSE-STACKED FLY
9. CRETAN

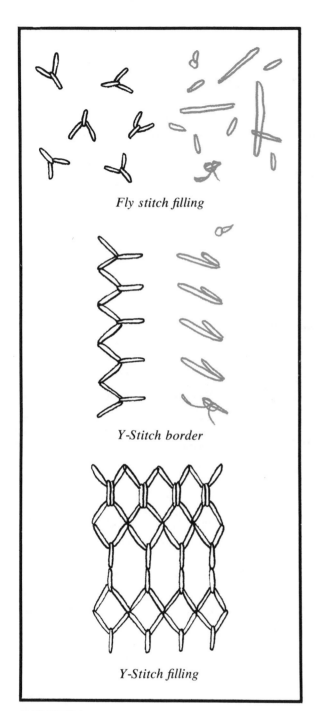

Fly stitch filling

Y-Stitch border

Y-Stitch filling

D.O.W. ↓

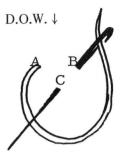

Step 1.   Bring thread up at A; pull through. Make a loop down and around to the right, insert needle at B, bring up at C and (loop beneath needle) pull through.

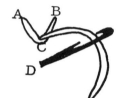

Step 2.   Insert needle at D; continue to next (nearest) stitch and repeat Step 1.

Y-STITCH BORDER

Work same as fly stitch. Notice that B is in the same hole for the first and second stitches. This stitch should be worked very evenly.

When working as filling stitch, complete one row across, right to left, then turn work around and work second row back (upside down). Variations of arrangement are shown in the box.

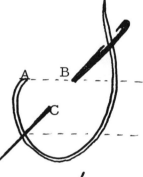

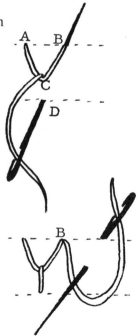

RHYTHM
Up / loop down—down—up /

USES
Fly can be used as a very light powdery filling, as buds (on a stem) or as seed pods (filled with seed stitch).

REMARKS
Fly stitch, with a shortened tack, is used in conjunction with many other stitches. For example, stacked fly can be used around a daisy when working double or triple daisies and the center becomes too crowded.

D.O.W. ↓

Step 1. Bring thread up at A; pull through. Make a loop, down and around to the right. Insert needle at B; bring up at C (loop beneath needle) and pull through.

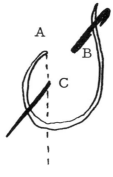

Step 2. Make loop down and around to the right. Insert needle at D; bring up at E, (loop beneath needle) and pull through. To finish stitch, tack stitch last loop at end of line.

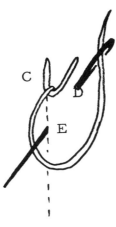

Note

For variations (1,2) of the stitch, make loops down and around to the left when open part of the loop is on the left.

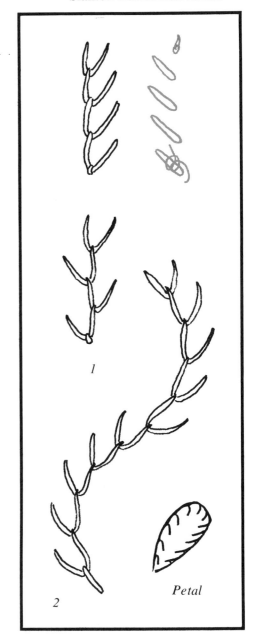

1

2   *Petal*

RHYTHM
Up / loop down and around to right—pull down over loop /

USES
Petals, wide borders.

REMARKS
Work loosely, especially on curves, or edge will "fall in." When necessary (on sharp curves), tack occasional stitches.

Step 1. Bring thread up at A; pull through. Make a loop down and around to the right, insert needle at B, bring up at C (loop beneath needle) and pull through.

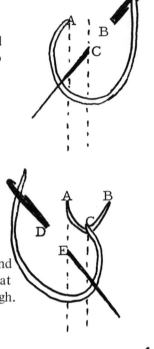

RHYTHM
Up / loop to right—down—up over loop / loop to left—down—up over loop /

USES
Fat flower stems, wide borders.

REMARKS
Great filling stitch when worked row after row. Try turning alternate rows upside down.

Step 2. Make a loop, down and around to the left; insert needle at D; bring up at E and (loop beneath needle) pull through.

Step 3. Make a loop down and around to the right. Insert needle at F, bring up at G (loop beneath needle) pull through. Continue, repeating Step 2. To finish tack stitch last loop.

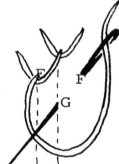

D.O.W. ↓

Step 1.   Bring thread up at A; pull through. Make loop, down and around to the right. Insert needle at B, bring up at C (loop beneath needle) and pull through.

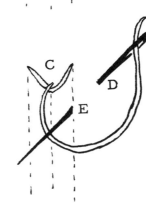

Step 2.   Make loop down and around to the right. Insert needle at D, bring up at E (loop beneath needle) and pull through.

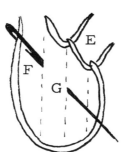

Step 3.   Make loop down and around to the left. Insert needle at F, bring up at G (loop beneath needle) and pull through.

Step 4.   Make another loop to the left, etc. Continue, making two loops to the right and two loops to the left, until end. Finish with tack stitch over last loop.

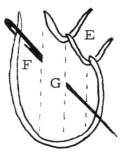

Plotting the stitch   Increased angle

RHYTHM
Up / loop down and around to right—down—up over loop / loop down and around to right—(again)—down—up over loop / down and around to left—down—up over loop / (twice)

USES
Wide decorative borders.

REMARKS
I used this stitch (in blue cotton floss) on all edges of receiving blankets and baby kimonos, when expecting my first child. Naturally I had a boy! Today's teenagers use it in bright colors along seams of blue jeans.

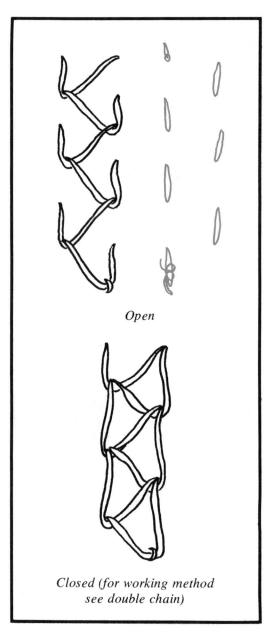

Open

*Closed (for working method
see double chain)*

D.O. W. ↓

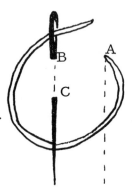

Step 1. Bring thread up at A; pull through. Make a loop, down and around to the left. Insert needle at B, bring up at C (loop beneath needle) and pull through.

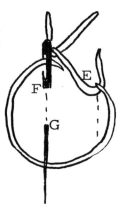

Step 2. Make a loop down and around to the right. Insert needle at D directly across from C, bring up at E (loop beneath needle) and pull through.

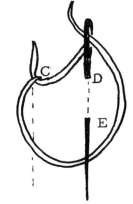

Step 3. Make loop to left and continue. Make one loop to the right and one to the left. To finish, tack stitch the last loop.

RHYTHM
Up / loop down and around to left—down—up over loop / loop down and around to right—down—up over loop /

USES
Broad lines, tree branches.

REMARKS
Covers both sides of parallel lines at same time, but will show some print line between stitches.

Note

For a more solid edge, D may be moved up closer to A, forming the closed vertical feather stitch. When D and A are in the same hole (inside the loop) and the length is doubled, the stitch then becomes closed.

D.O.W. →

Step 1. Bring thread up at A; pull through. Make a shallow loop down and around to the right. Insert needle at B, bring up at C (loop beneath needle) and pull through.

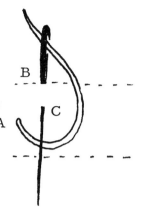

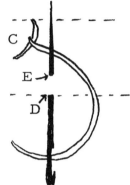

Step 2. Make a shallow loop down and around to the right. Insert needle at D, bring up at E (loop beneath needle) and pull through.

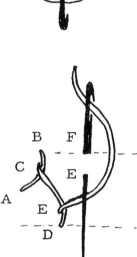

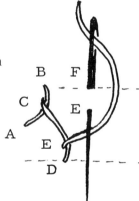

Faggot filling

Step 3. Repeat Step 1, keeping stitch F-G the same length and paralled with B-C. Filling stitch is worked from left to right, each row a separate journey. Stitches are placed in the same holes as row before.
(Fabric may be turned upside down for second journey.)

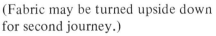

RHYTHM
Up / loop down and around to right—down—up over loop / loop down around to left—down—up over loop /

USES
Insertion stitch, used to join two pieces of fabric. Wide border stitch or filling, used in conjunction with outline, chain, etc.

REMARKS
This is like a Cretan stitch standing on its ear.

E.7 LONG-ARMED FEATHER STITCH
Stacked Feather Stitch

RHYTHM

Up / loop down and around to right
—down—up over loop / loop down and
around to right—down—up over loop /

USES

Leaves, feathers.

REMARKS

Don't pull stitches up too tightly; the
threads will curve gently and look like a
real feather. The "vein" of the leaf looks
like purling.

D.O.W. ↓

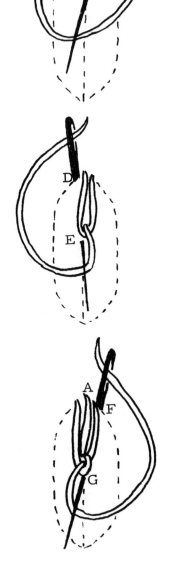

Step 1. Bring thread up at A; pull through. Make a loop down and around to the right. Insert needle at B, bring up at C and (loop beneath needle) pull through. Keep loop loose.

Step 2. Make a loop down and around to the left. Insert needle at D bring up at E and (loop beneath needle) pull through.

Step 3. Make a loop down and around to the right. Insert needle at F (very close to B), bring up at G and (loop beneath needle) pull through.

Note

This is a stitch which will follow a curvy pattern (such as a leaf) very nicely. When the center line is worked off to one side, the stitches will resemble a quill or feather. For clarity in diagramming, spaces are open to show individual stitches. For solid effect, no fabric should show at edges. Work stitches very close together

D.O.W. ↓

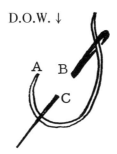

Step 1. Bring thread up at A; pull through. Make a loop down and around to the right insert needle at B bring up at C (loop beneath needle) and pull through.

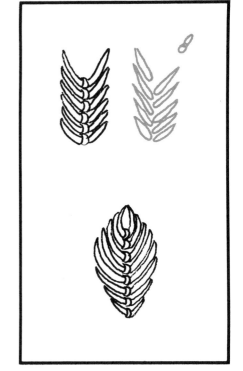

Step 2. Insert needle at D (one thread lower than C) bring up at E (one thread lower than A) and pull through.

RHYTHM
Up / loop down and around to right—down—up over loop / tack

USES
Leaves, petals.

Step 3. Continue as for Step 1. Each stitch is placed directly below stitch above so that no fabric shows through between stitches.

REMARKS
If a pointed leaf is desired, start at top point with a lazy daisy and work fly stitches around it.

Note

To fill a leaf shape work a single chain stitch first, then make fly stitches around it, widening to the middle of the area and then diminishing to keep shape at base. Do not pull loops up so tightly that curve of thread is lost.

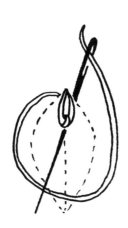

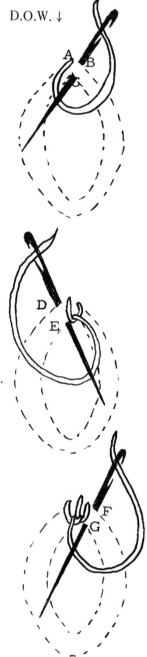

Step 1.   Bring thread up at A and pull through. Make a loop down and around to the right. Insert needle at B, bring up at C (loop under needle) and pull through.

Step 2.   Make a loop down and around to the left. Insert needle at D, bring up at E (loop under needle) and pull through.

Step 3.   Make loop to the right, insert needle at F, bring up at G, etc.

Stitches half completed illustrate how the angle of the needle flattens. The stitch remains small on the outside and the thread "weaves" across the center. Stitches may be worked closely or spaced widely.

RHYTHM
Up / loop down and around to right—down—up over loop / loop down and around to left—down—up over loop /

USES
Fat round or oval leaves, petals.

REMARKS
This stitch is particularly exciting when two shades of yarn are used in the needle at the same time.

Note

Open Cretan is worked with spacing between stitches giving a light and airy appearance. Closed Cretan is worked so closely that no fabric shows between stitches. This gives a heavy, solid stitch.

family F

CROSS STITCHES

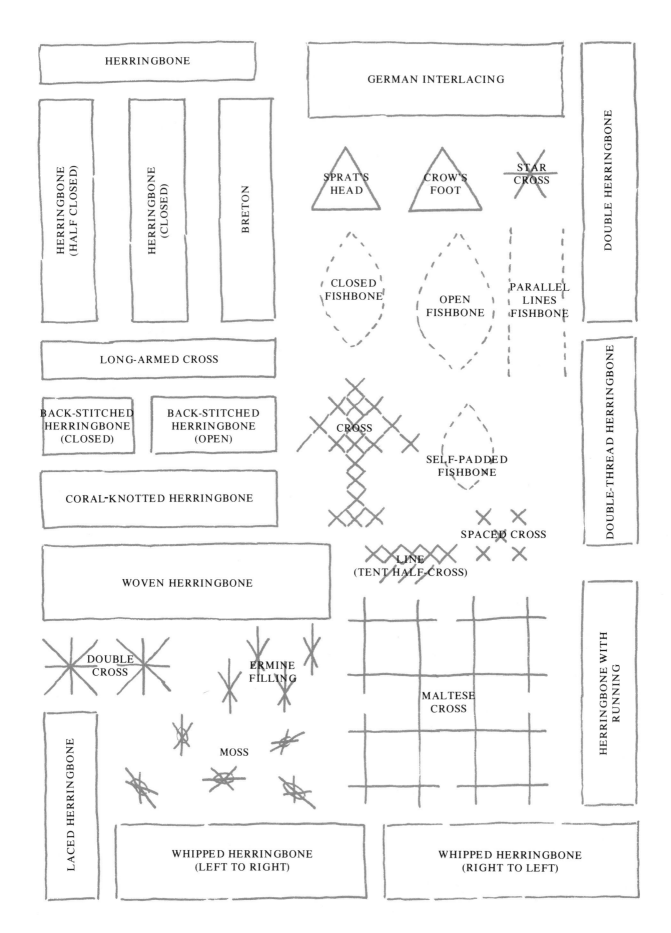

HERRINGBONE

HERRINGBONE (HALF CLOSED)

HERRINGBONE (CLOSED)

BRETON

GERMAN INTERLACING

DOUBLE HERRINGBONE

SPRAT'S HEAD

CROW'S FOOT

STAR CROSS

CLOSED FISHBONE

OPEN FISHBONE

PARALLEL LINES FISHBONE

LONG-ARMED CROSS

BACK-STITCHED HERRINGBONE (CLOSED)

BACK-STITCHED HERRINGBONE (OPEN)

CORAL-KNOTTED HERRINGBONE

CROSS

SELF-PADDED FISHBONE

DOUBLE-THREAD HERRINGBONE

SPACED CROSS

LINE (TENT HALF-CROSS)

WOVEN HERRINGBONE

DOUBLE CROSS

ERMINE FILLING

MALTESE CROSS

HERRINGBONE WITH RUNNING

LACED HERRINGBONE

MOSS

WHIPPED HERRINGBONE (LEFT TO RIGHT)

WHIPPED HERRINGBONE (RIGHT TO LEFT)

family F   Cross Stitches

Basic rhythm: up / down /   ✗

Progression of difficulty

Isolated   1. CROSS (Basic Stitch) AND FILLING
             2. DOUBLE CROSS, STAR CROSS
             3. MOSS STITCH
             4. SPRAT'S HEAD
             5. CROW'S FOOT

Line   6. LONG-ARMED CROSS (Plaited Slav)
             7. HERRINGBONE (Catch Stitch)
             8. DOUBLE HERRINGBONE
             9. BRETON

Stacked   10. FISHBONE
             11. SELF-PADDED FISHBONE

Grouped   12. ERMINE FILLING

Combined   13. BACK-STITCHED HERRINGBONE
             14. CORAL-KNOTTED HERRINGBONE (Tied Herringbone)
             15. HERRINGBONE VARIATIONS: HERRINGBONE WITH
                 RUNNING, LACED HERRINGBONE, WHIPPED
                 HERRINGBONE
             16. WOVEN HERRINGBONE
             17. MALTESE CROSS (Interlacing)
             18. GERMAN INTERLACING

F.1 CROSS STITCH AND FILLING

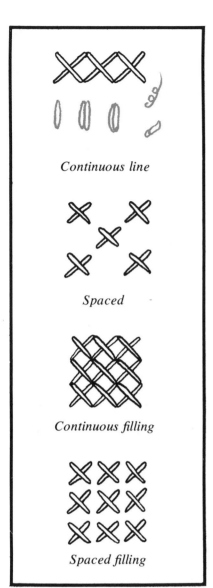

Continuous line

Spaced

Continuous filling

Spaced filling

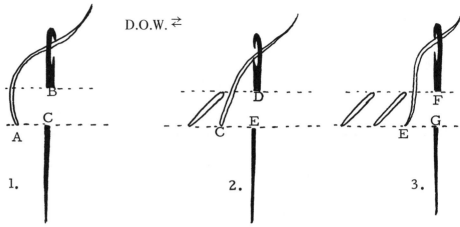

D.O.W. ⇄

1.   2.   3.

FIRST JOURNEY

Step 1.   Bring thread up at A; pull through. Insert needle at B, bring up at C; pull through.

Steps 2 and 3.   Continue, setting C-D and E-F, pulling thread through between each stitch.

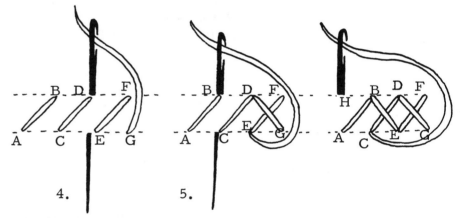

4.   5.

SECOND JOURNEY

Step 4.   Insert needle again at D, bring up at E; pull through. (Holes are the same.)

Step 5.   Continue until the line is covered.

Note

Remember that all lower (bottom) stitches cross in one direction; all upper (top) stitches cross in the other. For closed cross stitch, use the same holes on one side of the previous stitch; for open (or spaced) cross stitch use separate holes but keep straight lines.

RHYTHM
Up / down—up /
USES
Geometric shapes, straight lines, stylized flowers and leaves.
REMARKS
If you prefer to complete each stitch as you go along, use this rhythm (working from bottom up); up —lower left / to down upper right and up upper left / to down lower right / and back to beginning (at upper left), which will start new stitch. If you find you have set the base stitch in the wrong direction, cheat a little and slide the top stitch under before setting it.

D.O.W. Any

DOUBLE CROSS STITCH. Follow steps 1-4 and A-H in order. All four stitches cross at center point. A tack stitch worked at right angles with H-G will be necessary if stitches are long.

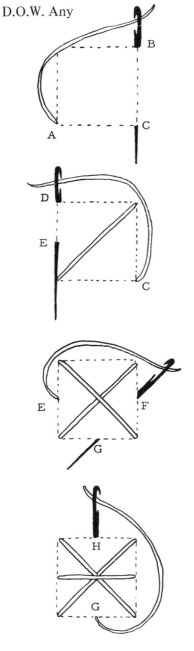

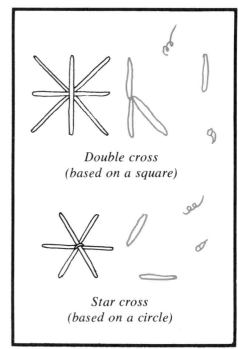

*Double cross
(based on a square)*

*Star cross
(based on a circle)*

RHYTHM
Up / down / up / down /

USES
Filling large geometric area, foundation stitch for whipping.

REMARKS
When setting this stitch in freehand, use "stab" method and set each stitch before starting the next.

STAR CROSS STITCH. Work same as above. All three stitches cross at center. A tack stitch at a right angle to last stitch will be necessary is stitches are long.

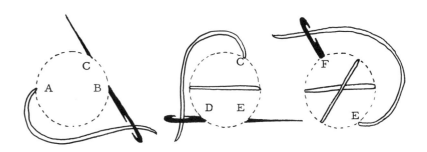

F.3 MOSS STITCH

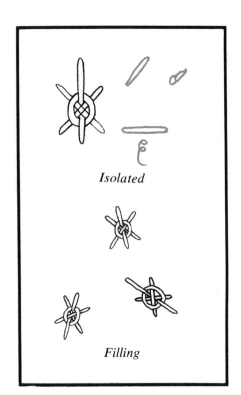

Isolated

Filling

RHYTHM
Up / down—up / twist loop—slide / tack

USES
Maple leaves, filling.

REMARKS
This stitch is my own invention. While doing a freehand autumn landscape "needle painting," I needed a stitch which would resemble maple leaves, and, in fooling around with it, developed this stitch. I'll share!

D.O.W. Any

Step 1. Bring thread up at A; pull through. Insert needle at B, bring up at C pull through.

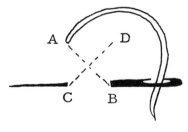

Step 2. Insert needle at D, bring up at E; pull through.

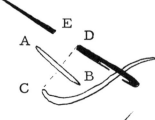

Step 3. Twist thread around to make loop; be sure loose end is underneath crossover. Hold in place with finger.

Step 4. Slide needle over loop, under cross stitch and over lower part of loop; pull through. Do not pierce fabric.

—DNPF

Step 5. Insert needle at F to complete stitch.

Note

Changing the length of the stitches adds variety and working with irregular spacing adds interest.

D.O.W. ↓

Step 1. Bring thread up at A; pull through. Insert needle at B, and, picking up one thread of fabric, bring out at C. Pull through.

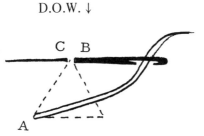

RHYTHM
Up / down—up / down—up /

USES
Arrow points, geometric shapes, raised stitches.

Step 2. Holding thread above needle, insert at D and bring up at E, very close to A. Pull through.

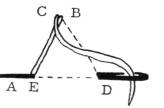

REMARKS
If sharper point is desired, place one straight stitch at top going down into triangle. All except the tip will be covered by subsequent stitches.

Step 3. Holding thread below needle, insert at F; bring up at G and pull through. Continue working Steps 2 and 3 until area is covered.

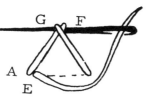

F.5 CROW'S FOOT STITCH

RHYTHM
Up / down—up / down—up /

USES
Raised arrowheads, fancy triangles.

REMARKS
An interesting weaving pattern de-velops as work progresses. Stitches are better defined in heavier yarn.

D.O.W. ↘

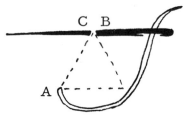

Step 1. Bring thread up at A; pull through. Insert needle at B, pick up one thread of fabric, bring needle up at C and pull through.

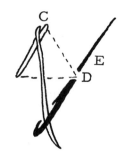

Step 2. Insert needle at D, pick up one thread of fabric, bring up at E; pull through.

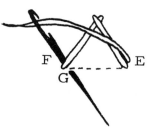

Step 3. Insert needle at F, bring up at G; pull through.

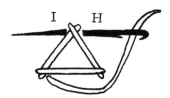

Step 4. Pick up slightly larger stitch (insert at H, up at I) and continue go-ing in a clockwise pattern. Each addi-tional stitch will be slightly larger than the one before, until entire triangle is filled.

Step 1. Bring thread up at A; pull through. Insert needle at B, bring up at C; pull through.

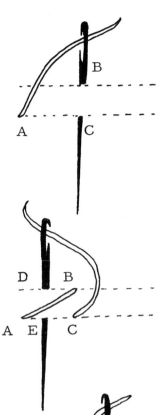

Step 2. Insert needle at D, bring up at E; pull through.

Step 3. Insert needle at F, bring up at G; pull through.

Step 4. Insert needle at B (same hole), bring up at C (same hole), pull through.

Note

Must be worked very evenly to produce correct effect.

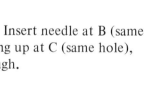

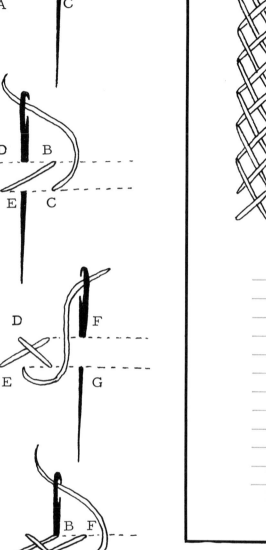

RHYTHM
Up / down—up / down—up /
USES
Wide borders, medium width, semi-solid lines.
REMARKS
Surprisingly quick and easy to work out, takes a little practice to keep even.

F.7 HERRINGBONE STITCH
Catch Stitch

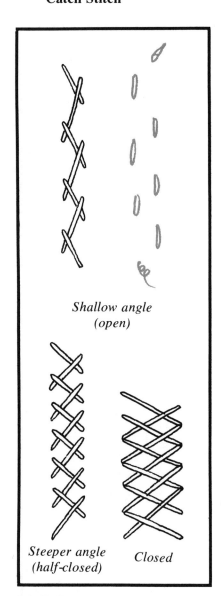

*Shallow angle
(open)*

*Steeper angle
(half-closed)*   *Closed*

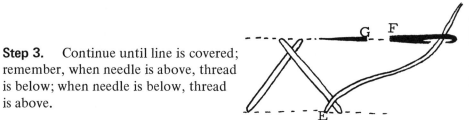

Step 1.   Bring thread up at A; pull through. Insert needle (on upper line) at B, bring up at C (thread is held below upper line) and pull through.

Step 2.   With thread above lower line, insert needle at D (on lower line), bring up at E and pull through.

Step 3.   Continue until line is covered; remember, when needle is above, thread is below; when needle is below, thread is above.

RHYTHM
Up / yarn below, needle above —down—up / yarn above, needle below—down—up /

USES
Wide decorative borders, hemming.

REMARKS
This is the stitch I use for hemming all my clothes. It gathers the lower fold gently and "floats" the hem over the fabric. Use sewing cotton double in needle when doing this.

RHYTHM
Part 1: up / yarn below, needle above
—down—up / yarn above, needle below
—down—up /
Part 2: up / slide needle under second
stitch of first journey—down—up / yarn
above, needle below—down—up /

USES
Wide decorative borders, broad lines.

REMARKS
A truly beautiful stitch. Be sure contrast in
color is strong enough to show off effect.

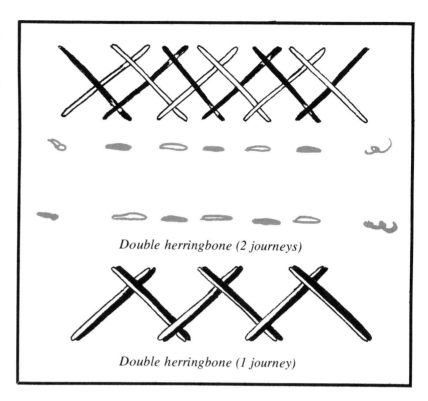

Double herringbone (2 journeys)

Double herringbone (1 journey)

Learn Herringbone stitch first (see F.7).

D.O.W. →

Step 1.   Work foundation stitch, starting at A.

Step 2.   With contrasting color, bring thread up at A; pull through. Insert needle at B, bring up at C; pull through. Slide needle under foundation stitch before stitch at D-E. Do not pierce fabric. The first dark stitches above show this completed; second dark stitches show needle in position. Spacing must be very even in both journeys.

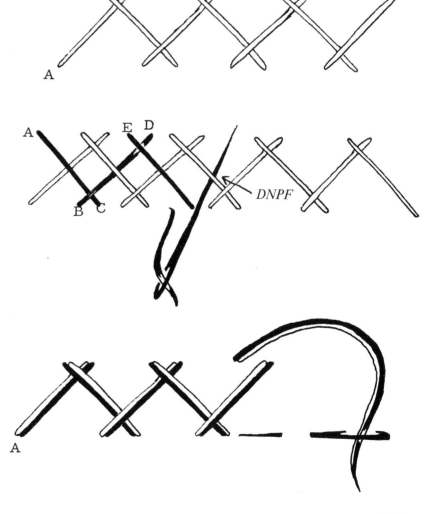

DOUBLE-THREADED HERRING-BONE. Thread two contrasting threads through the needle at the same time. Work as regular herringbone stitch. Twist thread in hole so that dark thread is always below light thread, or so that colors alternate.

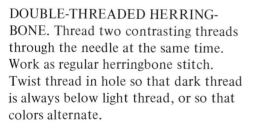

119

F.9 BRETON STITCH

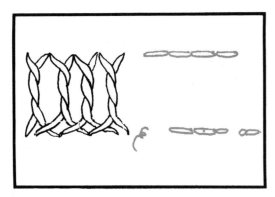

RHYTHM
Up / down—up / yarn above—slide / down /
USES
Very wide border stitch.
REMARKS
Works best on a straight line but can be worked in a circle; increase length of stitch at top.

D.O.W. →

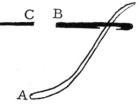

Step 1. Bring thread up at A; pull through. Insert at B, bring up at C; pull through.

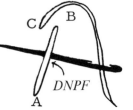

Step 2. Holding thread above, slide needle under stitch A-B and pull through gently. Do not pierce fabric.

Step 3. Insert needle at D, bring up at E, pull through. Continue with Steps 1 and 2. (A becomes E, B becomes F and C becomes B.) Note spacing at lower edge, making "legs" cross over.

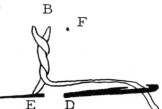

D.O.W. ↓

Step 1. Bring thread up at A; pull through. Insert needle at B, bring up at C and pull through. (This completes a straight stitch to make a pointed shape.)

Step 2. Insert needle, from right to left, at D; bring up at E and pull through.

Step 3. Insert needle at F (right to left), bring up at G; pull through. (This is the top of the stitch, which will continue to be almost horizontal but will increase in length as the shape increases and decrease as the shape decreases.)

Step 4. Insert needle at H, bring up at J; pull through. (This is the bottom of the stitch which remains the same length all the way down.)

Note

When working on two parallel lines, slant both top and bottom of stitch. Follow the A,B,C's; C and B are covered by next stitch.

Open

Closed

Open
(worked on 2 parallel lines)

RHYTHM
(After straight stitch) up top left / yarn above, needle below—down—up / yarn below, needle above—down top right and up again left /

USES
Leaves, petals of flowers.

REMARKS
This is the herringbone stitch "'stacked up" instead of running along in a line—quick and easy!

F.11 SELF-PADDED FISHBONE STITCH

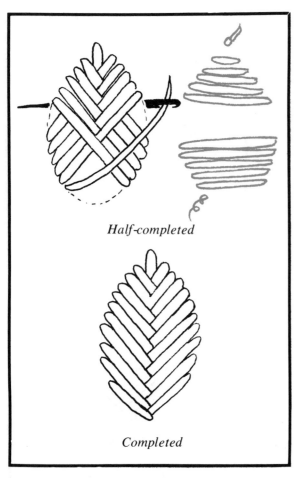

Half-completed

Completed

RHYTHM
Up / yarn above—down—up / yarn below—down—up /

USES
Raised thick leaf shapes, fat flower petals.

REMARKS
The lower part of this stitch is hard to keep even. It has a tendency to fall off.

D.O.W. ↓

Step 1. Bring thread up at A; pull through. Insert needle at B, bring up at C; pull through. (This makes a straight stitch which gives a point on the tip of the leaf shape.)

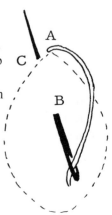

Step 2. Insert needle at D, bring up at E; pull through. Notice that points D and E (and all lower points) are slightly *inside* line to be covered.

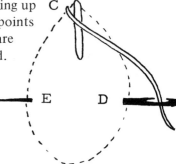

Step 3. Insert needle at F, bring up at G; pull through. Notice that all upper points are slightly *outside* of line to be covered.

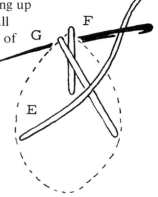

Step 4. Continue working bottom and top of each stitch until area is covered.

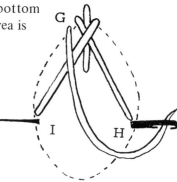

D.O.W. ⇄

Step 1.   Bring thread up at A; pull through. Insert needle at B, bring up at C; pull through.

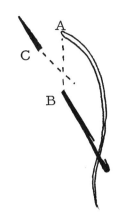

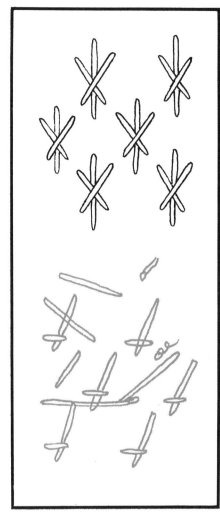

Step 2.   Insert needle at D, bring up at E; pull through.

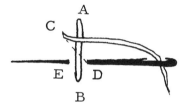

Step 3.   Insert needle at F (completes first stitch); bring up at G (like A of first stitch) and pull through.

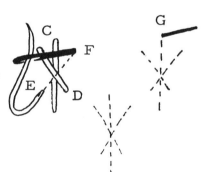

Note

Proper spacing is very important with this stitch. C and F should be wider apart than E and D. The second row will overlap the first so that crosses form straight, diagonal lines.

RHYTHM
Up / down—up / down—up / down

USES
Scattered filling, regular pattern filling.

REMARKS
If a large area is to be filled, begin at lower right corner and work up to the left so that the back doesn't become too messy!

123

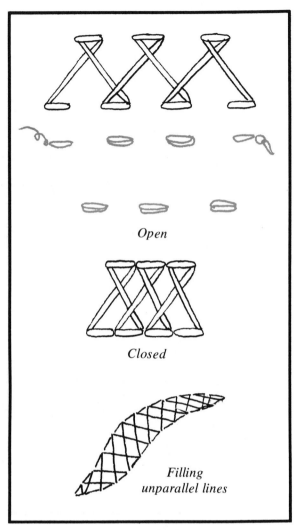

Open

Closed

*Filling
unparallel lines*

Step 1. Bring thread up at A; pull through. Insert needle at B, bring up at C; pull through.

D.O.W. →

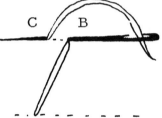

Step 2. Insert needle again at B (same hole), bring up at C (same hole) and pull through.

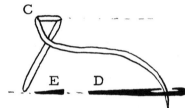

Step 3. Insert needle at D, bring up at E; pull through.

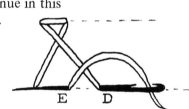

Step 4. Insert needle again at D, bring up at E; pull through. Continue in this manner until line is covered.

RHYTHM
Up / down—up / down—up /

USES
Wide borders.

REMARKS
When worked over printed parallel lines, remember, the line will show between stitches.

Note

To work this stitch closed (so that C-B, E-D, etc. form a solid line), place that part of the stitch closer and come up through the same hole at the right end.

RHYTHM
Part 1: up / yarn below, needle above—down—up / yarn above, needle below—down—up /
*   Part 2: up / C-loop—down—up /*

USES
Wide borders, raised stitches.

REMARKS
After mastering this stitch, try whipping around foundation stitch between knots for candy cane effect.

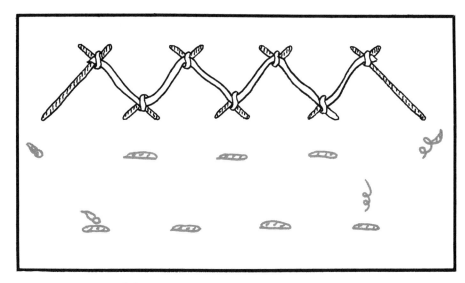

D.O.W. → and ← 2 Journeys

Work foundation stitches (see herringbone stitch, F.7).

Step 1. Bring contrasting thread up at A; pull through. Make a loop down and around to the right. Without piercing the fabric, slide the needle under the first cross of foundation stitch and, with lower part of loop beneath the needle, pull knot thus formed snug.

Step 2. Repeat first step at second stitch (lower line). Continue working in a zig-zag line until foundation stitches are covered. At end insert needle close to last knot, pull through to the back and knot off.

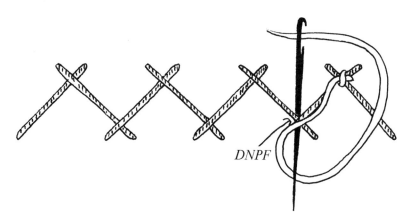

F.15 HERRINGBONE STITCH VARIATIONS

RHYTHM
*Part 1: up / yarn below, needle above—
down—up / yarn above, needle below
—down—up /*
  Part 2: varies with each one.

USES
Wide decorative borders.

REMARKS
When herringbone is worked across a
very wide area, a tacking stitch (at inter-
sections) should be used. For instance,
the running stitches could go in the other
direction.

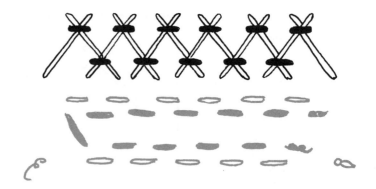

Herringbone with back or running stitch

Note

Set foundation stitches (see F.7).
With contrasting thread lace or whip
stitches as shown. Needles A and B
show position and order of work.

D.O.W. →

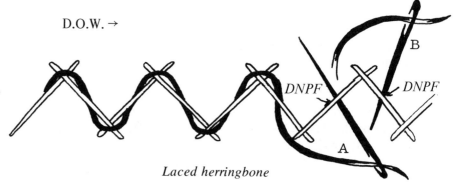

Laced herringbone

Whipped herringbone (left to right)

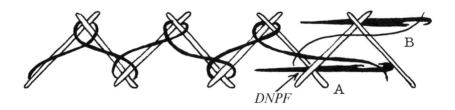

Whipped herringbone (right to left)

RHYTHM
Up / yarn below, needle above
—down—up / yarn above, needle
below—down—up /

USES
Wide decorative borders.

REMARKS
Only the foundation stitch will show
on the back; all the weaving takes
place on the surface. This stitch is
of German origin.

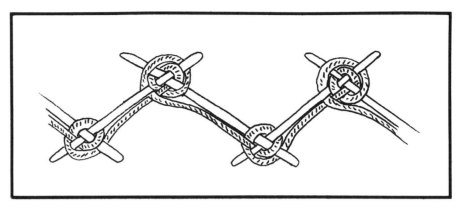

D.O.W. →

Lay foundation stitch (see herringbone
stitch, F.7) but slide needle *under*
each stitch so that cross-overs are
reversed.

←DNPF

Note

An easier way of setting foundation
stitches is to turn the work around so
that the top is now the bottom; work
herringbone in the regular manner.
Then turn work back, so that the top
is again on top, and proceed with
lacing, as shown, starting at the left.

Weave contrasting thread in this order:

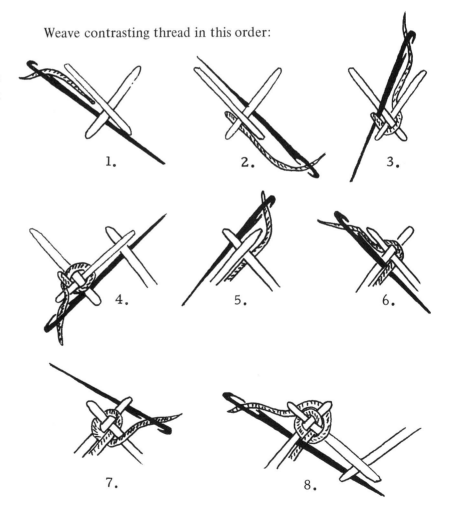

F.17 MALTESE CROSS STITCH
Interlacing Stitch

D.O.W. ⟷

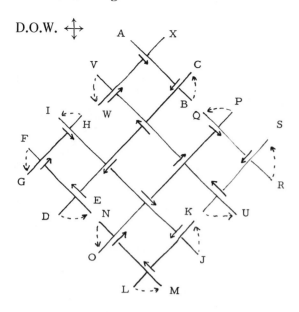

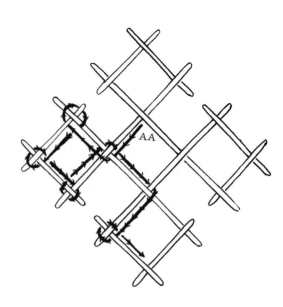

Step 1. Starting at A, work foundation stitches, following arrows and A,B,C, etc. Needle pierces fabric only at these points.

Step 2. Bring contrasting thread up at AA and weave in direction of arrows, until all crosses are woven.

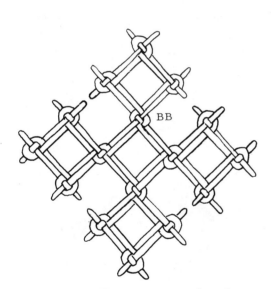

Step 3. Insert needle at BB and end off.

Note

A second journey of lacing, following exactly the same pattern, may be worked. Another variation is to work the second journey so that weaving is accomplished *over* where thread went *under* on first journey, etc.

RHYTHM
Up /.down—up /

USES
Large geometric shapes.

REMARKS
Lots of fun to do, but sketch in lines first, or baste them in with dark sewing thread which could be removed later.

RHYTHM
Part 1: up / yarn below, needle above —down—up / yarn above, needle below—down—up /
Part 2: same, but slide under on up stroke, weaving over, under, etc.

USES
Wide decorative borders.

REMARKS
Only foundation stitches will show on the back; all the weaving is done on the surface. Looks important, it could replace commercial trim on clothing!

Note

Be familiar with double herringbone before attempting this stitch.

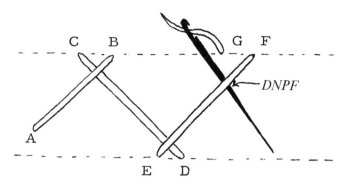

Step 1.   Work large herringbone, but note that thread is slipped under after working each top stitch.

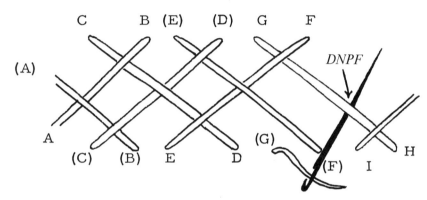

Step 2.   Note how threads cross at each intersection.

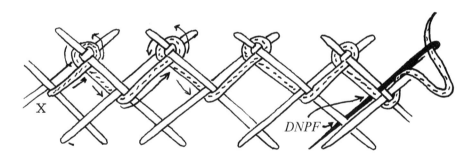

Step 3.   With contrasting thread, weave in counterclockwise direction. Second thread does not pierce fabric.

Step 4.   At right end, reverse direction and continue weaving lower and center crosses.

129

family G

KNOTTED STITCHES

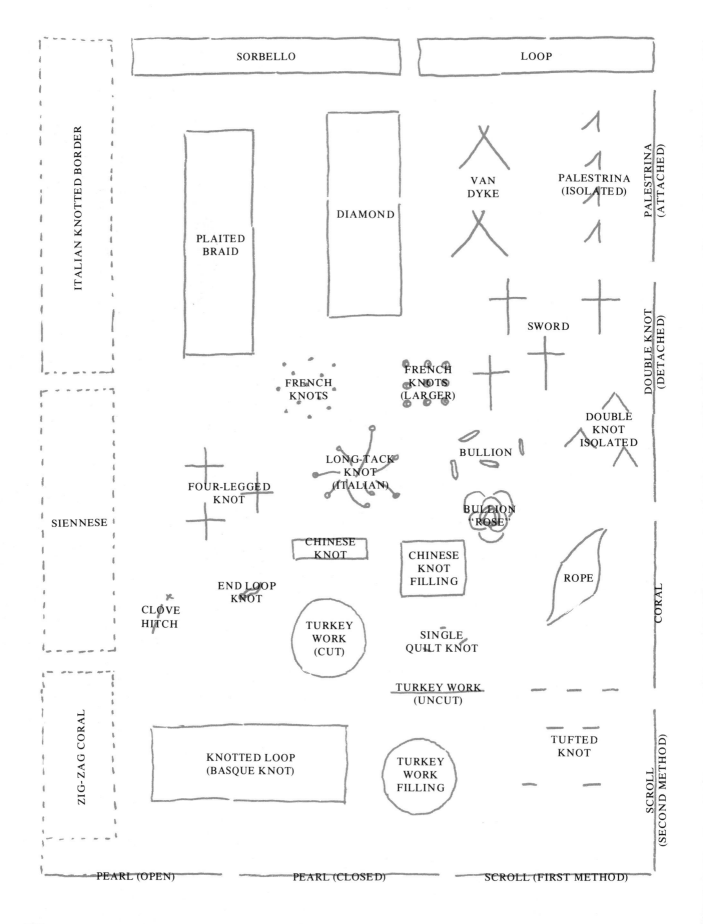

SORBELLO

LOOP

ITALIAN KNOTTED BORDER

PALESTRINA (ATTACHED)

VAN DYKE

PALESTRINA (ISOLATED)

PLAITED BRAID

DIAMOND

DOUBLE KNOT (DETACHED)

SWORD

FRENCH KNOTS

FRENCH KNOTS (LARGER)

DOUBLE KNOT ISOLATED

SIENNESE

FOUR-LEGGED KNOT

LONG-TACK KNOT (ITALIAN)

BULLION

BULLION 'ROSE'

CHINESE KNOT

CHINESE KNOT FILLING

ROPE

CORAL

END LOOP KNOT

CLOVE HITCH

TURKEY WORK (CUT)

SINGLE QUILT KNOT

TURKEY WORK (UNCUT)

TUFTED KNOT

ZIG-ZAG CORAL

KNOTTED LOOP (BASQUE KNOT)

TURKEY WORK FILLING

SCROLL (SECOND METHOD)

PEARL (OPEN)

PEARL (CLOSED)

SCROLL (FIRST METHOD)

132

family G   Knotted Stitches

Basic rhythm: up / wrap around needle—down /

Progression of difficulty

Isolated (Basic Stitch)   1. FRENCH KNOT

Variations
2. LONG-TACK KNOT (Italian Knot)
3. FOUR-LEGGED KNOT
4. BULLION
5. SWORD
6. DOUBLE KNOT (Danish Knot)
7. CORAL
8. SCROLL
9. ROPE (Knotted Satin)
10. CHINESE KNOT
11. PEARL
12. ITALIAN KNOTTED BORDER
13. LOOP (Centipede)
14. VAN DYKE
15. SIENNESE

Angled   16. ZIG-ZAG CORAL

Grouped
17. PALESTRINA
18. TURKEY WORK (Quilt Knot, Tufted Knot)
19. FINISHING KNOTS: END LOOP, CLOVE HITCH
20. KNOTTED LOOP (Basque Knot)
21. SORBELLO
22. PLAITED BRAID
23. DIAMOND

G.1 FRENCH KNOTS

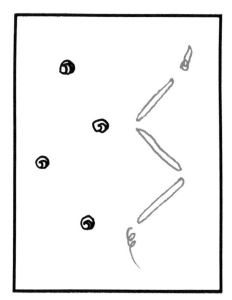

D.O.W. Any

Step 1. Bring thread up at A; pull through. Holding thread about two inches away from A, lay needle on top of thread as shown.

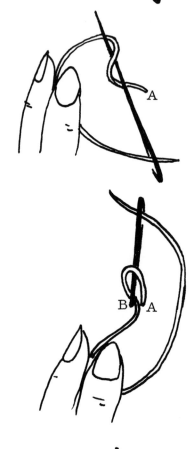

RHYTHM
Up / wrap around, down—tight /

USES
Flower centers, tiny flowers such as forget-me-nots, eyes of tiny animals or birds.

REMAKRS
Sliding the knot down the needle is very important to tighten the knot. Too much loop will result if you are not careful about this. Practice!

Step 2. Wrap thread once around needle as shown.

Step 3. Still holding working thread, insert needle in B (one fabric thread away from A.)

Step 4. Pull gently on thread so that knot slides down and is resting snug against fabric. Pull through.

Note

For a larger knot, use two or three threads in the needle at the same time. Another method, but not as satisfactory, is to wrap the yarn around the needle two or three times. It makes sloppy knots.

Learn French knot (G.1) first.

D.O.W. Any

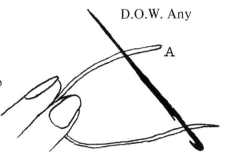

Step 1.   Bring thread up at A; pull through. Holding thread about two inches away from A, lay needle on top of thread as shown.

Step 2.   Wrap thread once around needle as shown.

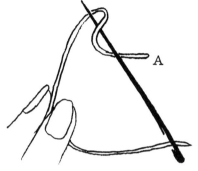

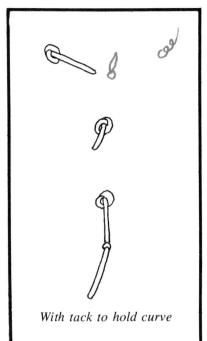

With tack to hold curve

Step 3.   Insert needle at B, a short distance from A but in any direction. Slide knot down needle by pulling on working thread so the knot is sitting on the fabric, and pull needle through.

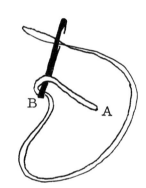

RHYTHM
Up / wrap around—move over—down—slide knot down /

USES
Flower centers, flower petals.

REMARKS
This is a most useful stitch. It can be arranged in a "wheel" to form the base of a flower by adding whipping around center; or it can be used as a tacking stitch in square couching. See I.10.

Note

If a very long curving tack is desired, use a tack or two to hold it in place.

G.3 FOUR-LEGGED KNOT STITCH

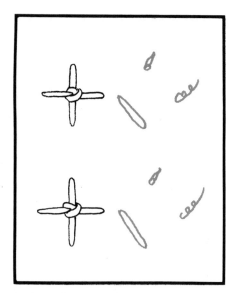

RHYTHM

Up | down—up | loop down and around—slide under—pull up loop —down |

USES

Isolated stitch or filling. Line up to make an interesting border stitch.

REMARKS

Leave the center knot loose for best effect.

D.O.W. Any

Step 1. Bring thread up at A; pull through. Insert needle at B, bring up at C; pull through.

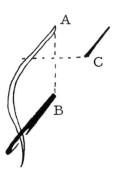

Step 2. Holding thread to the left, make a loop down and around to the right. Without piercing the fabric, slide needle under stitch and working thread, and over loop; pull through.

Step 3. Insert needle at D and pull through to the wrong side.

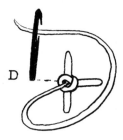

Step 1. Bring thread up at A; pull through. Insert needle at B, bring up again at A, but do not pull through.

D.O.W. Any

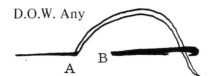

Step 2. Lay work flat so that both hands are free. Press down on eye of needle with middle finger of right hand and press index finger of right hand against the side of the point of the needle. With left hand, grasp thread about two inches from A and wrap thread around needle six or eight times, holding "wraps" in place with index finger.

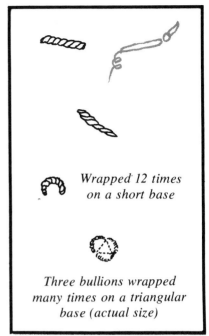

Wrapped 12 times on a short base

Three bullions wrapped many times on a triangular base (actual size)

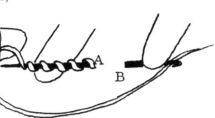

Step 3. Pinch needle and wrapping between thumb and index finger of right hand and push needle through. Continue pulling needle and thread through with left hand toward the left until thread is pulled all through.

Step 4. Then pull all the way to the right making sure that loops are not twisted on the thread.

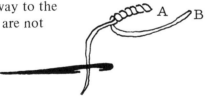

Step 5. Insert needle again at B and pull through. If wrapping is twisted, pull up stitch with eye of needle and straighten. Keep pulling on thread beneath fabric until wrappings are even.

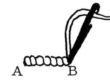

Note

This stitch takes patience and practice to perfect but it is well worth the effort. Do not wrap so tightly around the needle that it is hard to pull through; the coils will tighten when pulled in place.

RHYTHM
Up / down—up—needle point out, but not pulled through—wrap around / pull down to left and then right —adjust—down /

USES
Raised, important knots; flowers or buds.

REMARKS
This one takes some patience to perfect, but it is worth it. If you make a mistake when learning, cut it out, don't try to undo it. Try two contrasting colors in the needle at the same time.

For a beautiful "rose," work three bullions in dark red on tiny triangle, then three larger ones in lighter shades around those. Each subsequent round should be larger, so wrap second round about 10 times, third about 15 times. Try it!

G.5 SWORD STITCH

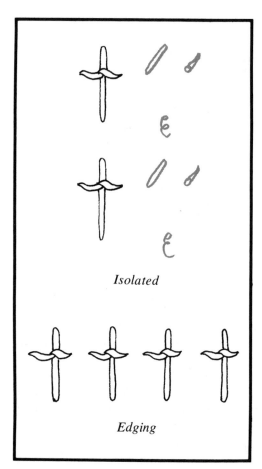

Isolated

Edging

RHYTHM
Up / down—up / slide under—down /

USES
Isolated, tacked for couching, lined up for border.

REMARKS
Don't pull first (diagonal) stitch too tightly or stitch will pucker.

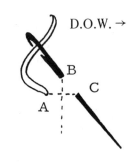

Step 1. Bring thread up at A; pull through. Insert needle at B, bring up at C; pull through loosely.

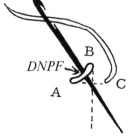

Step 2. Slide needle under stitch A-B in direction shown. Do not pierce fabric. Hold working thread above stitch. Pull through.

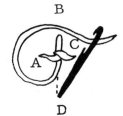

Step 3. Insert needle at D; end off. Length from B to D should be about twice as long as A to C.

Note

This stitch is very effective when used with trellis couching to tack down crossed threads.

D.O.W. →

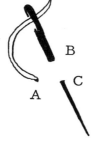

Step 1.   Bring thread up at A; pull through. Insert needle at B, bring up at C; pull through.

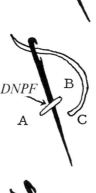

Step 2.   Slide needle under stitch (do not pierce fabric); pull through.

DNPF

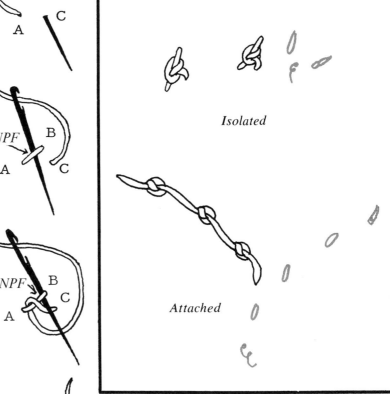

Isolated

Attached

Step 3.   Make a loop down and around to the right. Slide needle under stitch (left of B), over thread (left of C) and over loop; pull through.

DNPF

Step 4.   (For isolated stitch only.) Tack loop down; pull thread through to back and repeat Step 1.

RHYTHM
Up / down—up / slide under / slide under and over / down /

USES
As isolated stitch, forms tiny scattered flowers. (Use with feather stitch, for example.)

REMARKS
Keep knot loose for best effect.

Step 5.   (For attached stitch only.) Work Steps 1, 2 and 3. Omit Step 4 and repeat Step 1, starting at B-C.

G.7 CORAL STITCH

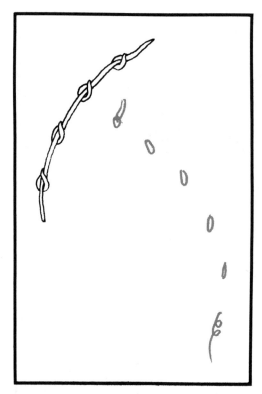

Step 1. Bring thread up at A; pull through. Make a loop over the line to be covered, and down and around to the right. Hold this loop in place with left thumb. Insert needle at B, bring up at C (making a small slanting stitch) and, with lower part of the loop beneath the needle, pull through.

D.O.W. ✓

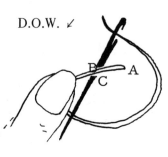

Step 2. Continue, always making a C-shaped loop and picking up both the thread and the line until line is covered.

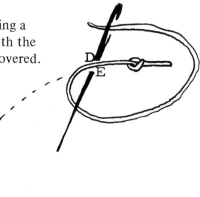

RHYTHM
Up / loop down and around to right—pick up line and thread /

USES
Bumpy lines.

REMARKS
Remember, C for coral and C for shape of loop as you work.

Elongated on the slanted stitch, it becomes twisted chain—can you see it?

Note

The amount of thread between knots may be lengthened or shortened; if line forms a tight curve work knots closer together.

D.O.W. →

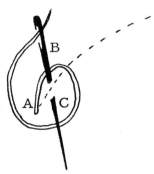

Step 1. Bring thread up at A; pull through. Make a loop, up and around to the right and down to the left. Insert needle (inside loop) at B, bring up at C, and, thread beneath needle, pull through.

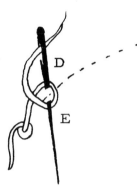

Step 2. Continue; take small, slanted stitches inside loops. Notice that the loop is pulled tight around the needle before pulling through. This helps to keep loop even when completed.

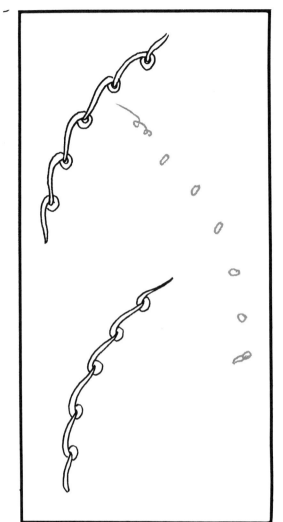

Step 3. This stitch may be worked from right to left. The effect is somewhat flatter when complete.

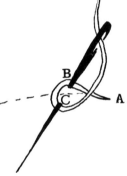

RHYTHM
Up / loop down and around to right—push loop away from line and pick up just the line—wrap thread tightly around needle /

USES
Stems, bumpy lines.

REMARKS
Don't pull this one up too tightly. It may stay in place, but it won't look the way it should.

141

G.9 ROPE STITCH
Knotted Satin

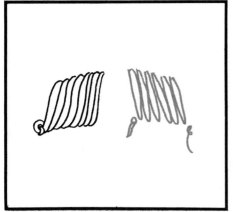

RHYTHM
Up / down—up—wrap thread around /
USES
Wide borders, thick stems.
REMARKS
This stitch gives a lovely rolling raised edge on lower side, a great three-dimensional effect. Stitches form a soft S-shape.

Step 1. Bring thread up at A; pull through. Make a loop down and around to the right. Insert needle at B, bring up at C (very close to A). Loop beneath needle, pull through.

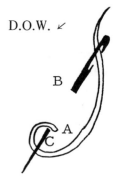

D.O.W.

Step 2. Work second stitch in the same manner, very close to the first. Continue to end of line. Finish by tacking last loop down.

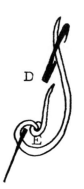

Step 1. Bring thread up at A; pull through. With left hand, grasp thread near A and twist a loop as shown, holding in place with thumb.

D.O.W. ←

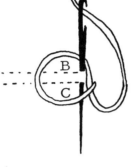

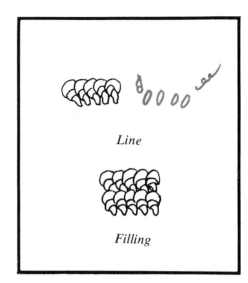

Line

Filling

Step 2. Still holding loop with thumb, insert needle at B (inside loop) and bring up at C so that thread is *above* needle.

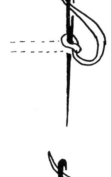

RHYTHM
Up / twisted loop—down—up—tighten
USES
Raised lines, decorative borders.
REMARKS
Want to have some fun? At step 2 let loop be under needle at both top and bottom of needle and then pull loop up tight. You've invented a whole new stitch!

Step 3. Pull loop up snug around needle. Pull through.

Step 4. Repeat Steps 1, 2, and 3, working *second* stitch very close to first. To end, do not come up again at C, just pull through.

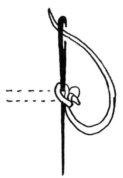

Note

When working filling, *second* row is again worked from right to left with point B staggered between A and C of *first* row.

G.11 PEARL STITCH

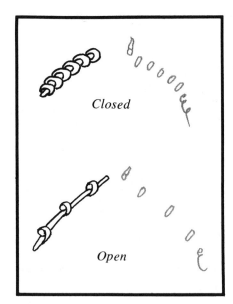

Closed

Open

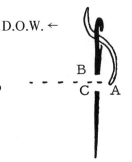

D.O.W. ←

Step 1.   Bring thread up at A; pull
through. Insert needle at B, bring up at
C and pull through, leaving a small loop
of thread between A and B.

Step 2.   With left thumb holding
working thread down in position, slide
needle under the loop from left to
right as shown. Do not pierce fabric.
Then swing the needle to the right and
slide the point under the working
thread.

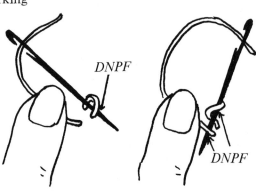

Step 3.   Holding the working thread
in position, pull the needle down
through the loop to set stitch.

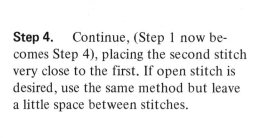

Step 4.   Continue, (Step 1 now becomes Step 4), placing the second stitch
very close to the first. If open stitch is
desired, use the same method but leave
a little space between stitches.

(Work French knot (G.1) first.

Step 1.   Bring thread up at A; pull through. Make a loop down and around to the right. Insert needle at B, bring up at C. Loop beneath needle, pull through.

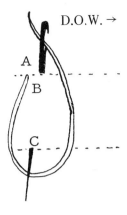

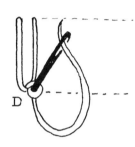

Step 2.   Lay needle on top of thread close to C, and wrap thread once around needle. Insert needle at D (outside loop), pull knot down on needle and pull through.

Step 3.   Work second stitch in the same manner, very close to the first stitch.

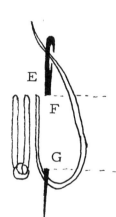

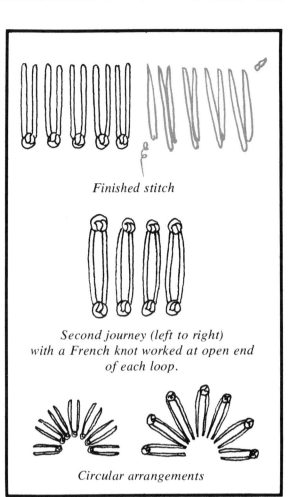

Finished stitch

Second journey (left to right) with a French knot worked at open end of each loop.

Circular arrangements

RHYTHM
Up / loop down and around to right—down—up / wrap—down—slide /

USES
Wide borders, variety of textures.

REMARKS
If you think of a daisy (or fly) stitch with the Italian knot (long tack knot) used as the tack stitch, it will make this one very simple.

145

G.13 LOOP STITCH
Centipede Stitch

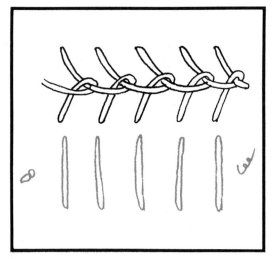

RHYTHM
Up / down—up / thread to left, slide under stitch

USES
Wide border stitch, could be stem of plant with tiny French knot flowers at end of each "branch."

REMARKS
Concentrate on keeping loops at center; it goes to one side very quickly.

D.O.W. ←

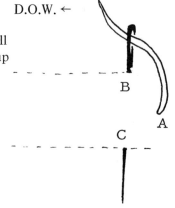

Step 1. Bring thread up at A; pull through. Insert needle at B, bring up at C; pull through.

Step 2. Holding thread up and around to the left, slide needle under stitch A-B (do not pierce fabric) over working thread, and pull through loosely.

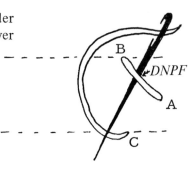

Step 3. Keeping the center loop halfway between the line, continue until line is covered.

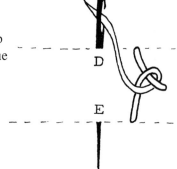

D.O.W. ↓

Step 1.   Bring thread up at A; pull through. Insert needle at B, bring up at C and pull through.

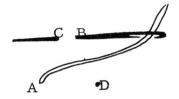

Step 2.   Insert needle at D, bring up at E and pull through.

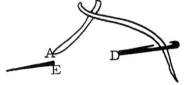

Step 3.   Slide needle under X (where threads cross); do not pierce fabric. Pull through loosely. Insert needle at F, bring up at G (just below E) and continue picking up only the last X worked.

DNPF

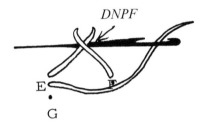

Note

The needle pierces the fabric only on the top of the first stitch and the bottom of all stitches. All tops, after the initial one, are slipping through between X's and fabric.

X's have a tendency to slip down, so when the needle is in position 3, push up toward the top of the stitch and hold stitches with left thumb while setting the last part of the stitch at F.

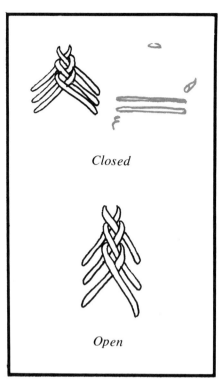

Closed

Open

RHYTHM
Up / down—up / down—up / slide under X—pull up—down /

USES
Leaf shapes with veins, petals, wide borders.

REMARKS
This stitch takes some practice. It works best with heavy thread.

G.15 SIENNESE STITCH

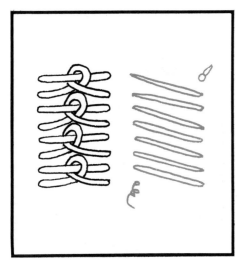

RHYTHM
Up / down—up / slide under, then over and down—up /

USES
Very wide decorative borders.

REMARKS
Very quick and easy to do, with lovely raised effect. Covers wide lines nicely.

D.O.W. ↓

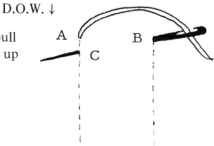

Step 1. Bring thread up at A; pull through. Insert needle at B, bring up at C; pull through.

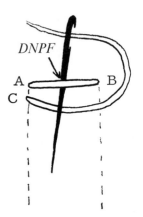

Step 2. Make a loop down and around to the right. Slide needle under straight stitch (A-B) from top to bottom, and, needle over loop, pull through loosely. Do not pierce fabric.

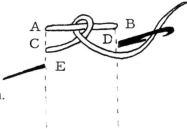

Step 3. Insert needle at D, bring up at E; pull through. Continue, working a straight stitch and then loop stitch until area is covered. Tops of loops should touch bottom of previous stitch.

Work coral stitch (G.7) first.

Step 1. As with coral stitch, starting on the top line, bring thread up at A; pull through. Make a loop down and around to the right, insert needle at B, bring up at C. With loop beneath needle pull through.

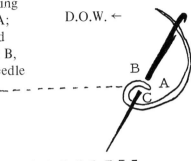

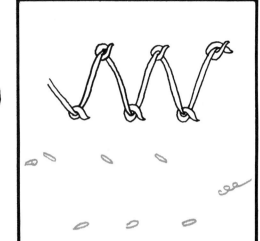

RHYTHM
Up / C-loop—down—up / reverse C-loop —down—up /

USES
Very wide borders.

REMARKS
Spacing and angles can make this stitch look very different. Try variations.

Step 2. (Loop on lower line is reversed.) Bring thread down to cross lower line; make loop up and around to the right; hold in place with left thumb. Insert needle at D, bring up at E, and, with loop beneath needle, pull through. Continue with Step 1 on upper line, etc.

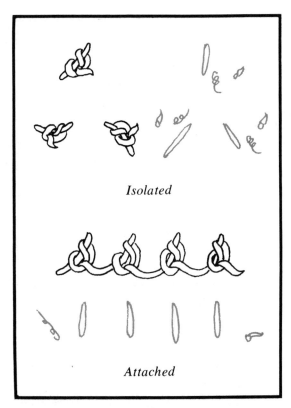

Isolated

Attached

RHYTHM
Up / down—up / loop—slide under and over /
loop—slide under and over /

USES
Isolated stitches, filling stitches, wide important borders.

REMARKS
The knot formed across the basic stitch is a clove hitch!

D.O.W. →

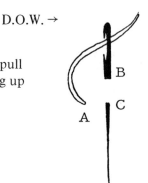

Step 1. Bring thread up at A; pull through. Insert needle at B, bring up at C, pull through.

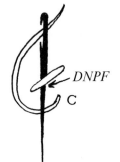

Step 2. Make a loop down and around to the left. Slide needle under stitch (do not pierce fabric), over loop, and pull through.

Step 3. Make another loop down and around to the left. Slide needle under stitch again, over loop, and pull through. For isolated stitch, tack down loop and continue with Step 1.

Step 4. For attached stitch, do not tack last loop. Insert needle at D and continue with Step 1. Tack last stitch at end of line.

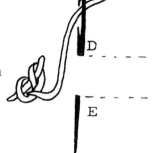

Step 1.   From the top of the fabric (no knot) insert the needle at A, bring up at B, and pull through leaving about a half inch of yarn sticking up on the surface of the fabric.

D.O.W. Any

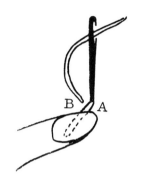

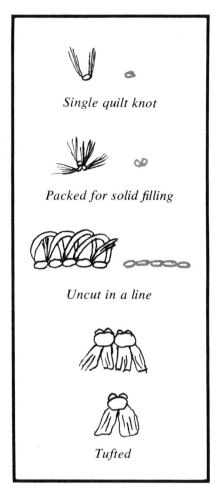

Single quilt knot

Packed for solid filling

Uncut in a line

Tufted

Step 2.   Holding loose end down with thumb, insert needle again at A; pull through. Bring up at B, pull through.

Step 3.   Knot may be cut (one half inch from fabric) at this point or next stitch started without cutting. If loops are to remain uncut, work loops over little finger or a pencil to keep uniformity.

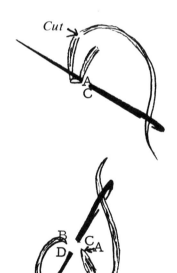

Step 4.   Tufted knot: work the same way as above but make C-D cross A-B underneath. As the loop is pulled up, make sure the loose end at A is within the loop, then cut to match other end.

RHYTHM
Down / but leave end sticking up—up / down again (same hole) / up again (other end) / cut off

USES
Dandelion "puffs," cattails, flower centers. Massed for full puffy effect. Used for knotting quilts.

REMARKS
The varieties of effect with this stitich, cut or uncut, are limitless, When packing for solid filling, hold loose ends away with left thumb so they won't pull through with next stitch. Work from the bottom of area to top or from center out to edges.

Note

It is easier to work this stitch upside down. The finished diagram shows the stitch turned around.

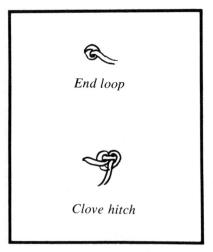

End loop

Clove hitch

REMARKS
Use knots only when there is no solid area in which to fasten ending threads. Whenever possible, weave the threads through the backs of stitches, over and under about three times, then repeat over last stitch (like a back stitch) and weave a couple more times.

D.O.W. Any

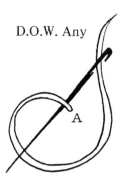

ONE LAZY WAY

Holding a loop down with thumb, slide needle under thread very close to A. Pull through loop and slide loop down close to fabric as it tightens. Cut off close to knot.

BEST METHOD

Turn embroidery to back. Make a loop as shown. Slide the needle under nearest stitch and bring up through the loop. Pull hard to the left. Make another loop in the opposite direction. Slide needle under the same stitch but from the other direction and pull thread through. Pull hard to the left again. (Knot will loop like a pretzel.) Cut off close to knot.

Note

The back of these knots will be the face or right side of the embroidery.

Work loop stitch (G.13) first.

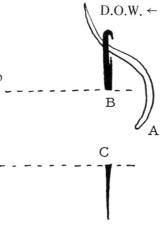

Step 1. Bring thread up at A; pull through. Insert needle at B, bring up at C, pull through.

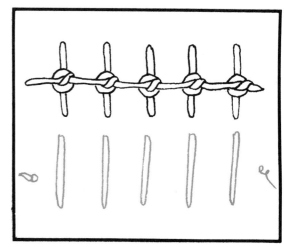

Step 2. Holding thread up to the left, slide needle under stitch A-B and pull through loosely. Do not pierce fabric.

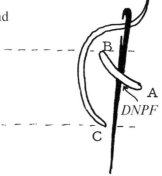

RHYTHM
Up / down—up / loop, slide, tighten, opposite loop, slide, tighten /

USES
Wide decorative borders.

REMARKS
Just add one more knot to loop stitch and you have this pretty variation.

Step 3. Make a loop down and around to the left. Slide needle under stitch A-B (to the left of first loop) and, with loop beneath needle, pull through.

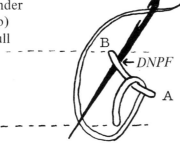

Step 4. Continue with Step 1. The knot should be pulled up firmly. (See completed figure.)

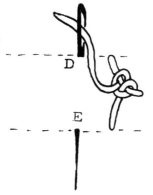

G.21 SORBELLO STITCH

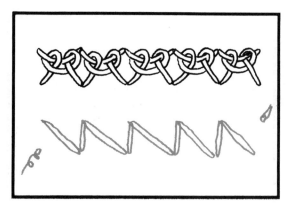

RHYTHM
Up / down—up / loop around—slide—loop around—slide—down—up /

USES
Wide decorative borders.

REMARKS
Just a clove hitch over the top straight stitch. Don't pull too tightly.

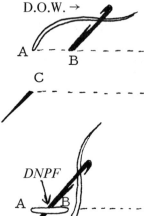

Step 1. Bring thread up at A; pull through. Insert needle at B, bring up at C; pull through.

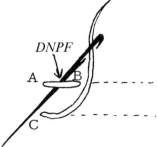

Step 2. Slide needle under stitch A-B (do not pierce fabric) and pull through loosely.

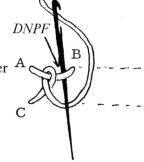

Step 3. Make a loop down and around to the right. Slide needle under stitch A-B, to the right of first loop, and over loop. Pull through loosely.

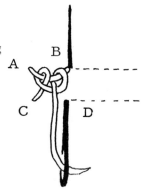

Step 4. Insert needle at D and bring up again at B. Pull through. Continue with Step 1.

D.O.W. ↓

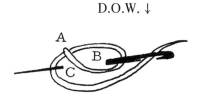

Step 1. Bring thread up at A; pull through. Twist a loop in the thread as shown. Insert needle at B and bring up at C; pull through, leaving a loop.

Step 2. Slide needle under crossed threads. Do not pierce fabric. Leave a loose loop.

DNPF

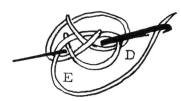

Step 3. Insert needle at D, bring up at C (inside loops as shown); pull through, leaving loop.

RHYTHM
Up / twist loop—down—up / slide / loop around—down—up /

USES
Very decorative wide borders.

REMARKS
Practice this one. The loops are difficult to keep even, but it's fun to do.

Step 4. Slide needle under last cross-over of loops but over all other threads. Pull through, leaving loop.

DNPF

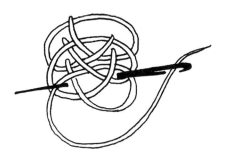

Step 5. Same as Step 3. Continue, working Steps 4 and 5, alternately, sliding needle on 4, piercing fabric on 5.

G.23 DIAMOND STITCH

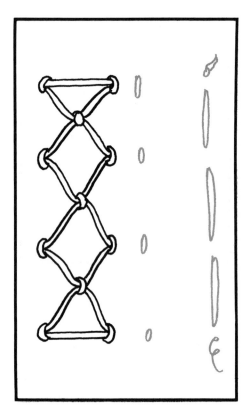

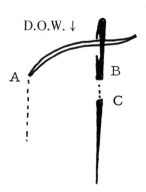

Step 1. Bring thread up at A; pull through. Insert needle at B, bring out at C; pull through.

RHYTHM

Up / down—up / loop around on right —slide / loop around on left—slide / down —up / loop around middle—slide / down —up /

USES

Wide decorative borders.

REMARKS

Be careful of your tension; it's a hard stitch to keep even, but it is very beautiful! Try parallel rows to make a filling stitch.

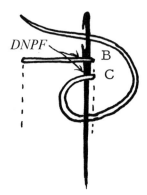

Step 2. Holding thread to the left, make loop down and around to right. Slide needle under first stitch, under working thread and over loop (do not pierce fabric); pull knot thus formed tightly to the right.

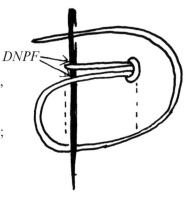

Step 3. Holding thread to the left, make loop down and around to the right. Slide needle under first stitch, under working thread and over loop; pull knot down to the left.

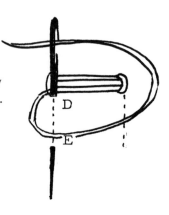

Step 4. Insert needle directly below left knot, bring out at E, pull through.

Step 5. Holding working thread to the right, make loop down and around to the left. Slide needle under working thread and over loop. Pull this knot straight down.

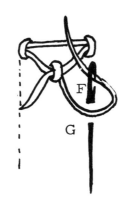

DNPF

Step 6. Insert needle at F, bring out at G (a tiny stitch) and pull through.

Step 7. Make knot as in Step 2. Continue.

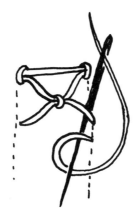

family **H**

COMPOSITE STITCHES

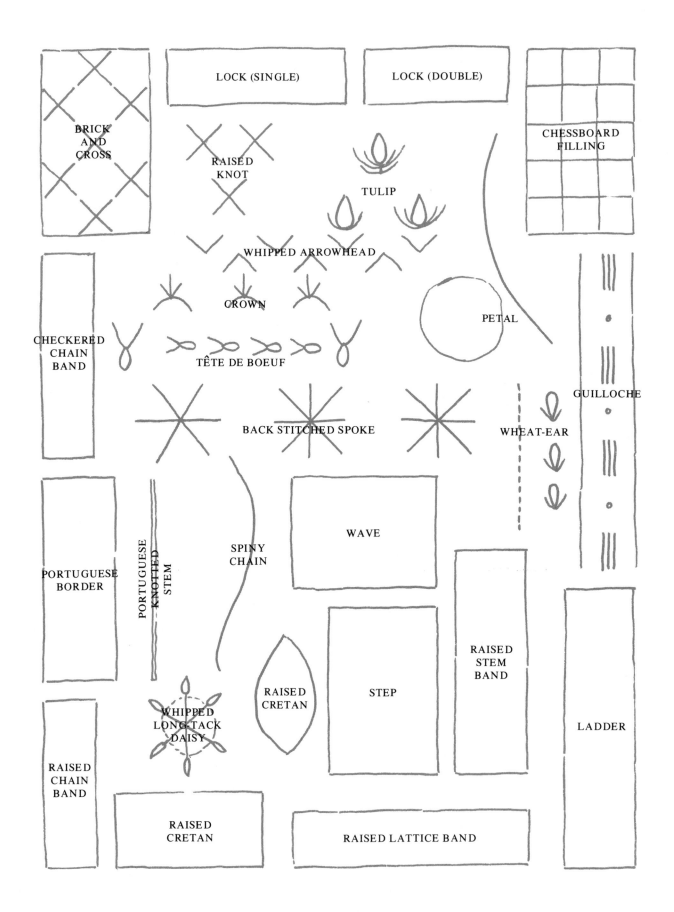

BRICK AND CROSS

LOCK (SINGLE)

LOCK (DOUBLE)

CHESSBOARD FILLING

RAISED KNOT

TULIP

WHIPPED ARROWHEAD

CROWN

CHECKERED CHAIN BAND

TÊTE DE BOEUF

PETAL

GUILLOCHE

BACK STITCHED SPOKE

WHEAT-EAR

PORTUGUESE BORDER

PORTUGUESE KNOTTED STEM

SPINY CHAIN

WAVE

RAISED STEM BAND

STEP

LADDER

WHIPPED LONG-TACK DAISY

RAISED CRETAN

RAISED CHAIN BAND

RAISED CRETAN

RAISED LATTICE BAND

family H Composite Stitches

Basic rhythm: same as component parts

In alphabetical order (no progression of difficulty)

1. BACK-STITCHED SPOKE (Back-stitched Star)
2. BRICK AND CROSS
3. CHECKERED CHAIN BAND
4. CHESSBOARD FILLING
5. CROWN
6. GUILLOCHE
7. LADDER
8. LOCK
9. PETAL
10. PORTUGUESE BORDER
11. PORTUGUESE KNOTTED STEM
12. RAISED CHAIN BAND
13. RAISED CRETAN (Figure Eight)
14. RAISED KNOT (Square Boss)
15. RAISED LATTICE BAND
16. RAISED STEM BAND (Raised Outline)
17. SLIPPED DETACHED CHAIN (Tulip)
18. SPINY CHAIN
19. STEP
20. TÊTE DE BOEUF (Head of the Bull)
21. WAVE STITCH FILLING (Huck Weaving)
22. WHEAT-EAR
23. WHIPPED ARROWHEAD (Raised Chevron)
24. WHIPPED LONG-TACK DAISY

H.1 BACK-STITCHED SPOKE STITCH
Back-stitched Star Stitch

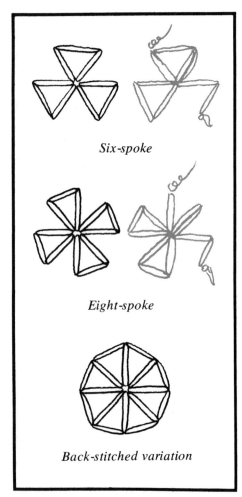

Six-spoke

Eight-spoke

Back-stitched variation

D.O.W. Any

Eight-spoke

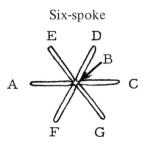

Step 1. Bring thread up at A; pull through. Insert needle in center (B) and bring up at C; pull through. Working in order (D, E, etc.) helps to divide spaces evenly.

Six-spoke

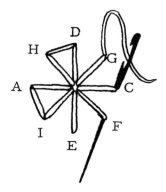

Step 2. Bring thread up at I (F in six-spoke) and pull through. Insert at A, bring up at H (E) and pull through. Continue until each group is connected.

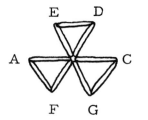

Note

A completely enclosed circle is an interesting variation. Outside stitches should be backstitches, although Holbein stitch may be used.

RHYTHM
Up / down / up / down /

COMPOSITION
Even numbers of straight stitches arranged in a wheel, connected in pairs with straight stitches.

USES
Isolated stitches, stylized flowers, geometric shapes.

REMARKS
Quick and easy. Can be further decorated with French knots between triangles, in center, or whipped around outside. Following A, B, C in order helps to place stitches when working freehand. It is not all that important if you have drawn design first.

D.O.W. ↓

Step 1. Work four satin stitches forming a perfect square. Stitches may be separated if thin thread is used.

A   B
C   D
E   F
G   H

Step 2. Bring thread up at I; pull through. Insert needle at J, bring up at K, pull through.

G   H
I
K   J

Step 3. Insert needle at L, bring up at M, pull through. M will now become A in Step 1. Continue working vertical rows, alternating cross and brick stitches as shown.

L

M

Variation

RHYTHM
Up / down—up /

COMPOSITION
Satin stitches with cross stitches.

USES
Filling geometric shapes.

REMARKS
Neatness counts. If this stitch is not done perfectly evenly, it looks terrible!

Note

Many variations may be used. Alternate direction of "bricks" in second row and/or use contrasting color for cross stitch.

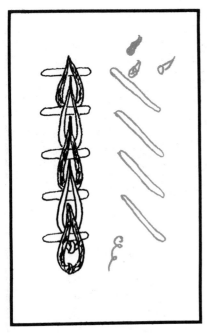

D.O.W. ↓

Step 1. Lay foundation of straight stitches. Thread two needles, one with dark and one with light thread. Bring thread halfway through needles and knot both ends together. With dark thread bring needle up above first stitch; pull through. With light thread, bring second needle up below first stitch. Separate first loop and bring light thread through this loop.

RHYTHM
Up / down—up /

COMPOSITION
Straight stitch with surface plaiting interlocking.

USES
Wide decorative borders.

REMARKS
Stitch looks best if darker shade is used in foundation stitch. It can be of a contrasting color, but keep the darkest and most intense shades on the foundation.

Step 2. Slide needle with dark thread under second stitch from top to bottom. Do not pierce fabric.

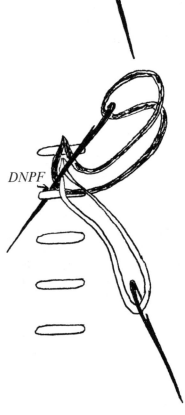

DNPF

Step 3. Bring dark thread through light loop. Slide needle with light thread under third stitch. Continue until all straight stitches are covered.

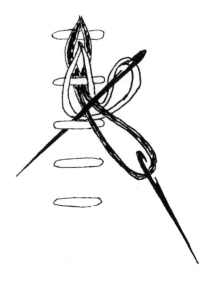

164

D.O.W. Any

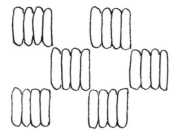

Step 1. Work foundation of four satin stitches in groups as shown.

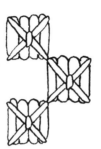

Step 2. Work a cross stitch over each satin stitch group. Tack the center down with a small straight stitch.

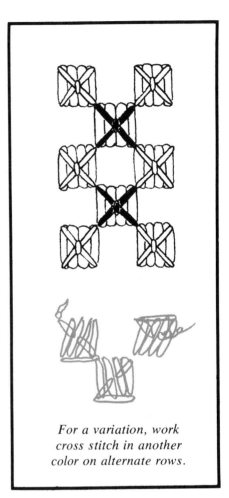

For a variation, work cross stitch in another color on alternate rows.

RHYTHM
Up / down—up /

COMPOSITION
Satin with tacked cross stitch.

USES
Dramatic area filling, very wide borders.

REMARKS
Keep even or effect is destroyed. Cross stitch and/or tacking may be of contrasting color.

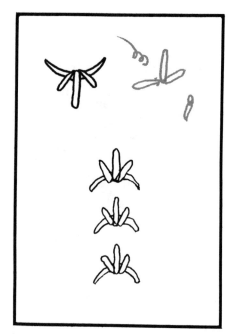

D.O.W. ↓

Step 1. Bring thread up at A; pull through. Make a loop down and around to the right, insert needle at B, bring up at C (loop beneath needle), and pull through. Keep loop loose to form a gentle curve.

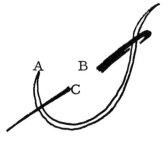

Step 2. Insert needle at D; bring up at C in the same hole but to the right of the working thread.

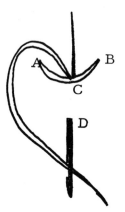

RHYTHM

Up / loop down and around—down—up / (over loop) down—up / down—up / down—up /

COMPOSITION

Fly stitch plus two straight stitches.

USES

Isolated, grouped for filling, arranged in flower shapes.

REMARKS

Keep tension loose on first part so that the curve will be gentle, without a hard "corner" at center.

Step 3. Insert needle at E, bring up at F and pull through. (Stitches C-E and C-F are the same length but both are shorter than C-D.)

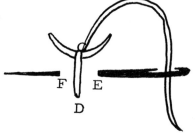

Step 4. Insert needle again at C but to the left of the two stitches already there. Continue at A of next stitch.

RHYTHM
*Up / down—up / (lacing) up / slide
—turn—slide*
COMPOSITION
*Satin, threading, with outline stitch
and French knots.*

USES
Wide borders, area filling.

REMARKS
*This traditional stitch may be var-
ied by the use of tête de bœuf to
replace the French knots, for example, and any narrow line stitches
along the outside borders.*

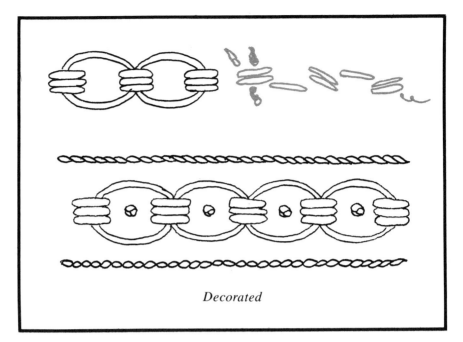

Decorated

D.O.W. →

Step 1. Work groups of three satin
stitches in a row, with spaces and
stitches equal in length.

Step 2. With contrasting color, bring
thread up at A; pull through. Slide
needle under second group from top
to bottom (do not pierce fabric); pull
through. Slide needle from bottom to
top under next group; lace subsequent
groups alternately, top to bottom,
bottom to top.

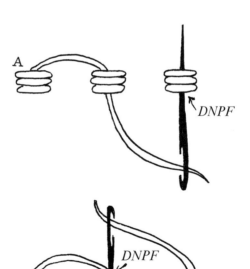

Step 3. Reverse direction and
continue, lacing in the opposite manner
to the beginning.

Note

Although stitch is complete with these
three steps, it is prettier when decorated with outline stitch on both sides
and a French knot worked in circles
formed by threading.

167

H.7 LADDER STITCH

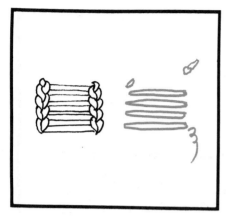

RHYTHM
Up / down—up / down—up / left—slide / right—slide / down—up /

COMPOSITION
Reverse chain with straight stitch.

USES
Wide borders.

REMARKS
A very pretty, neat stitch. Fills wide spaces easily and the raised edges give a nice finishing touch.

D.O.W. ↓

Step 1. Bring thread up at A; pull through. Holding thread below line, insert needle at B; bring up at C; pull through.

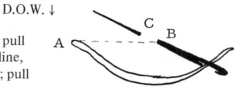

Step 2. Insert needle at D, bring up at E; pull through.

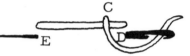

Step 3. Holding thread to the right, slide needle under stitch A-B (do not pierce fabric); pull through loosely.

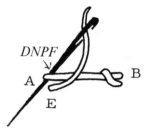

Step 4. Holding thread below first stitch, slide needle under stitch A-B, and under C above A-B. Pull through loosely.

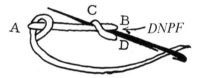

Step 5. Insert needle at F, bring up at G; pull through.

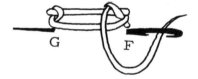

Step 6. Slide needle under loop above; pull through loosely. Continue, working reverse chain stitch on each side with straight stitch between. Finish on right side of stitch.

168

RHYTHM
Up / down / up /
COMPOSITION
Straight stitches with lacing.

USES
Wide borders, highly decorative edges.

REMARKS
Color combinations can make or break this one. Make sure shades are not so close that they lose impact.

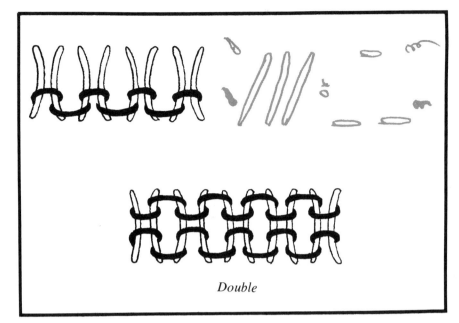

Double

D.O.W. →

Step 1. Lay foundation of straight stitches, following A,B,C etc.

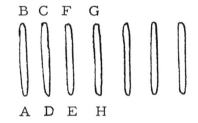

B C F G

A D E H

Step 2. With contrasting thread, bring needle up at AA; pull through. Holding thread above, slide needle under C-D and pull up firmly. Do not pierce fabric.

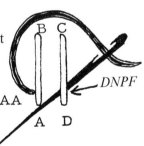

B C

DNPF

AA

A D

Step 3. Holding thread below, slide needle under E-F and pull through loosely. Continue lacing in this manner until all straight stitches are covered.

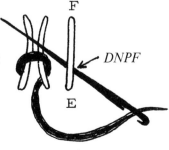

F

DNPF

E

Note

To double lace, turn work around and work the other side.

169

H.9 PETAL STITCH

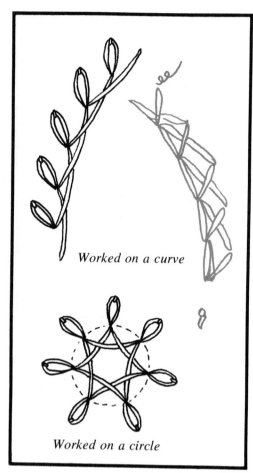

Worked on a curve

Worked on a circle

RHYTHM
Up / down—up / loop—down—up / tack

COMPOSITION
Outline and detached chain.

USES
Wonderful for flowers, fancy stems.

REMARKS
The greater the curve, the more interesting the overlapping stitches. Do not work too small. If circle is desired, do not draw pattern first; stitches will not cover. Better to take a coin, baste-stitch around it, and pull out stitches when finished. Or work freehand.

Lazy man's way: work large outline and then come back and do the daisies. (Daisies won't tell!)

D.O.W. ↗

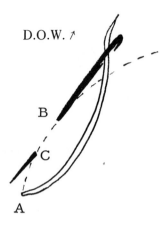

Step 1. Bring thread up at A; pull through. Holding thread below the line, insert needle at B, bring up at C; pull through.

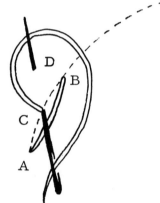

Step 2. Make a loop up and around to the right. Insert needle again at C, bring up at D, and loop beneath needle; pull through.

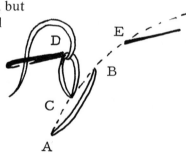

Step 3. Insert needle again at D, but outside of loop, bring up at E; pull through.

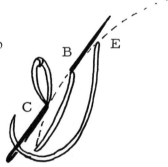

Step 4. Holding thread below the line, insert needle again at C, bring up again at B; pull through. Work next chain at B.

Note

When working circle, last stitch must be slipped under first to complete woven pattern.

D.O.W. ↑

Step 1.   Lay foundation stitches. Start at A, down at B, up at C, etc.

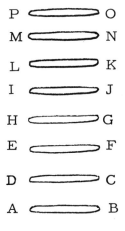

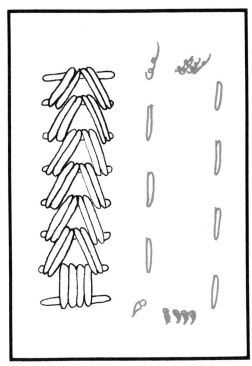

Step 2.   Bring thread up at AA. Holding thread to the right, slide needle under D-C and A-B, top to bottom, and pull through (do not pierce fabric). Slide needle under D-C only; pull through. Continue, always holding thread to the right, picking up two straight stitches (as shown) and one only (as at I-J) to top.

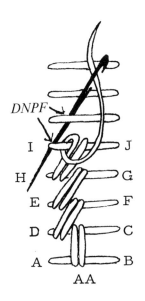

DNPF

AA

RHYTHM
Part 1: up / down / up / etc.
Part 2: up / slide / slide /

COMPOSITION
Straight stitches whipped with outline stitch which does not pierce fabric.

USES
Wide decorative borders.

REMARKS
Remember that foundation stitches do not cover parallel lines if drawn on material. Work freehand or baste, stitching in lines and pulling out basting after setting foundation stitches.

Step 3.   Work as for Step 2, but hold the thread always to the left of work.

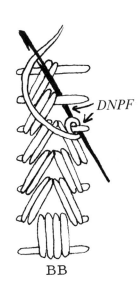

DNPF

BB

Note

Tension is important: keep outline stitch (whipping) loose enough so that straight stitches are not pulled out of line.

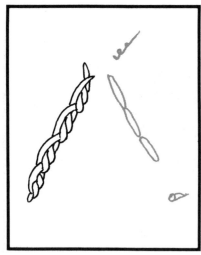

RHYTHM
Up / down—up / slide / slide /

COMPOSITION
Outline stitch whipped while in progress.

USES
Raised lines, medium heavy lines.

REMARKS
Remarkable show for such little effort.

D.O.W. ↗

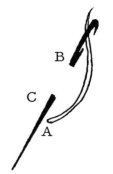

Step 1. Bring thread up at A; pull through. Holding thread to the right, insert needle at B, bring up at C; pull through.

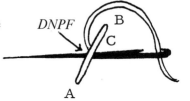

Step 2. Holding thread above, slide needle under A-B, between C and A. Do not pierce fabric.

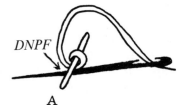

Step 3. Repeat Step 2. Be careful to keep second loop below first (closer to A).

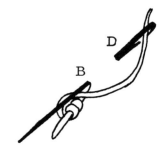

Step 4. Holding thread again to the right (as in Step 1), insert needle at D, bring up at B; pull through.

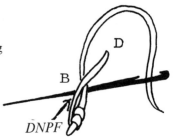

Step 5. Repeat Steps 2 and 3, sliding needle under two threads. Continue, alternately whipping (Steps 2 and 3) and working outline stitch (Step 5).

D.O.W. ↓

Step 1. Lay foundation of straight stitches or lay foundation of Roman chain stitches. This is desirable if parallel lines are printed and must be covered with embroidery.

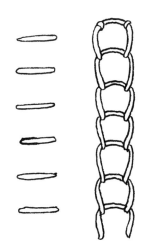

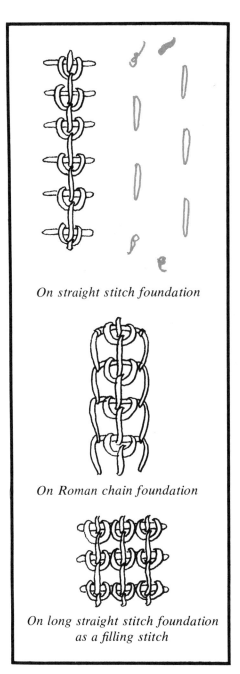

On straight stitch foundation

Step 2. Bring thread up at E; pull through. Slide needle under stitch A-B, from bottom to top; pull up loosely. Do not pierce fabric.

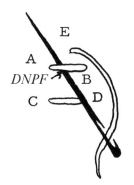

On Roman chain foundation

Step 3. Make a loop down and around to the right. Slide needle under stitch A-B to the right of E and, with loop beneath needle, pull through loosely. Continue, sliding needle under C-D as in Step 1, etc. End by tacking the last loop at end of row.

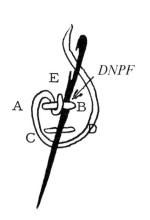

On long straight stitch foundation as a filling stitch

RHYTHM
Part 1: up / down /
Part 2: up / slide under / loop down and around—slide under /

COMPOSITION
Straight stitch or Roman chain with floating chain stitch.

USES
Raised borders, filling, medium to wide borders.

REMARKS
Do not pull loops too tightly; leave loose. Try working every other row (as a filling) upside down for different effect. Use contrasting colors for stronger effects.

H.13 RAISED CRETAN STITCH
Figure Eight Stitch

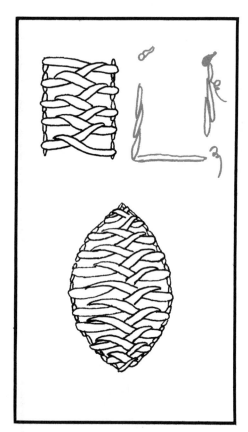

RHYTHM
Part 1: up / down /
Part 2: up / loop—slide / loop—slide /

COMPOSITION
Back stitch foundation with surface Cretan whipping.

USES
Wide borders, well-filled heavy lines, petals, leaves, etc.

REMARKS
Interesting effects happen when foundation is different in color or shade from lacing.

Step 1. Lay foundation stitches of small, even back stitches, the same number and across from each other on both lines (sides).

D.O.W. ↓

Step 2. Bring thread up at A; pull through. Holding thread down and around to the right, slide needle under first back stitch from right to left; pull through. Do not pierce fabric.

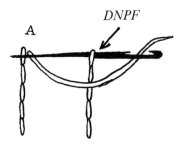

Step 3. Holding thread down and around to the left, slide needle under second stitch of left row from left to right. Do not pierce fabric. Pull through.

Note

Two or more stitches may be worked through each pair of back stitches to give a more solid effect. For variation: work left side over back stitches but work right side as regular Cretan. Most effective worked in a circle with back stitches in center.

D.O.W. Any

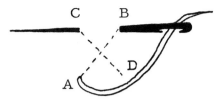

Step 1. Bring thread up at A; pull through. Insert needle at B, bring up at C; pull through.

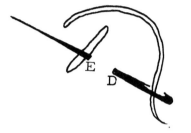

Step 2. Insert needle at D, bring up at E; pull through.

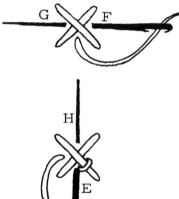

RHYTHM
Up / down—up / etc.

COMPOSITION
Cross stitch with back stitches.

USES
Arrange in pattern for filling, or use for bold, scattered, isolated stitches.

REMARKS
The order on which the back stitching is done is not important. Looks rather like the first round of whipping in raised spider web, but tension of loops can be controlled better this way.

Step 3. Insert needle at F, bring up at G; pull through.

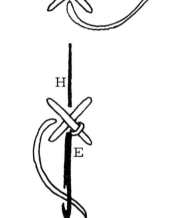

Step 4. Insert needle again at E, bring up at H; pull through.

Step 5. Insert needle again at G, bring up again at F; pull through.

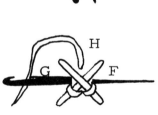

Step 6. Insert needle at H and pull through to complete stitch.

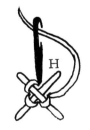

Note

This stitch may be used as isolated stitches for light filling, or may be arranged in a row as a border stitch. It may also be arranged as a checkerboard for a regular filling stitch.

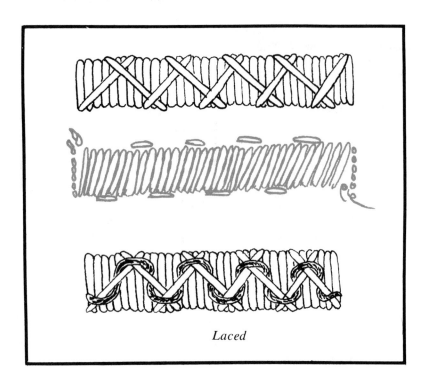

Laced

RHYTHM
Up / down—up /
COMPOSITION
Very long straight stitches covered by satin stitch and then covered by herringbone.
USES
Very heavy raised borders.
REMARKS
First straight stitches may be the same color as satin stitches as they do not show, but contrast is nice for herringbone.

D.O.W. Any

Step 1. Lay foundation of long straight stitches. If length is very long (over 10 inches) pin these threads in position.

Step 2. Work satin stitches over foundation so that foundation is completely covered. (See bar satin, B.14.)

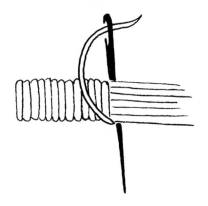

Step 3. Starting at A, work herringbone over satin stitches. Contrasting colors make design more interesting. Lacing the herringbone stitch with a contrasting color adds more interest. This produces a very raised stitch.

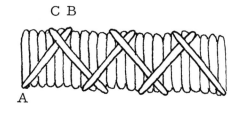

D.O.W. ↑

Step 1. Work straight stitches as shown. To make a more rounded effect, these may be worked over long vertical straight stitches, or several heavy threads may be slipped underneath after straight stitches are completed.

B

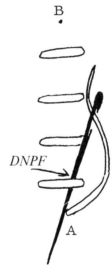

DNPF

Step 2. Bring thread up at A; pull through. Holding thread always to the right, slide needle under lowest stitch from top to bottom; do not pierce fabric. Continue, whipping each stitch to top. Insert needle at B; pull through and end off. Bring needle up again at A and continue whipping, always starting and ending in the same hole to give ends a rounded effect.

A

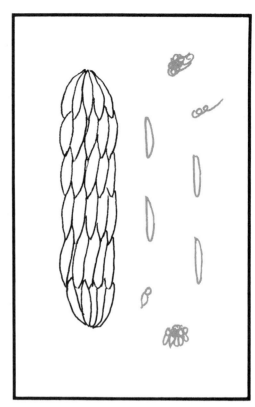

RHYTHM
Part 1: up / down—up /
Part 2: up / slide /

COMPOSITION
Straight stitch with whipping, which is worked as stem stitch.

USES
Very heavy wide lines, solid tree trunks, big branches, area filling (to look like a woven basket, for example).

REMARKS
Keep tension loose and even; works best with heavy yarns.

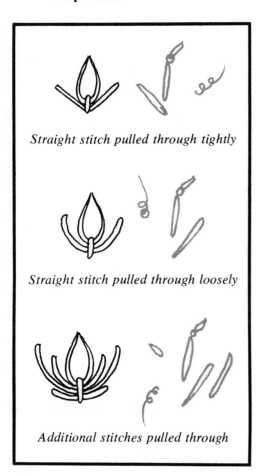

Straight stitch pulled through tightly

Straight stitch pulled through loosely

Additional stitches pulled through

RHYTHM
Up / loop down and around—down same hole—up over loop / down—up / slide / down

COMPOSITION
Chain with slipped straight stitch.

USES
Isolates stitches, spaced filling, flowers by themselves or arranged in circles.

REMARKS
After setting original daisy, try changing colors for the base stitches which are slid through.

D.O.W. ↓

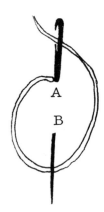

Step 1. Bring thread up at A; pull through. Make a loop down and around to the right. Insert needle again at A, up at B, and with loop beneath needle, pull through.

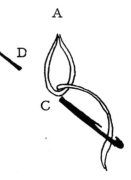

Step 2. Insert needle at C, bring up at D; pull through.

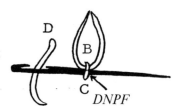

Step 3. Slide needle from left to right under tack stitch (B-C), do not pierce fabric, and pull through.

DNPF

Step 4. Insert needle at E and pull through to end off.

D.O.W. ↓

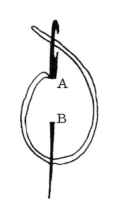

Step 1.   Bring thread up at A; pull through. Make a loop down and around to the right. Insert needle again at A, and with loop beneath needle, pull through loosely.

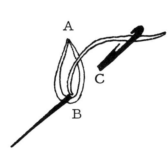

Step 2.   Insert needle at C, bring up again at B; pull through.

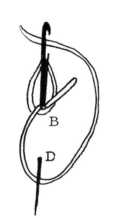

Step 3.   Make a loop down and around to the right, insert needle again at B. Bring up at D and, loop beneath needle, pull through loosely.

RHYTHM
Up / loop—down—up / down—up same hole /

COMPOSITION
Chain and straight stitch.

USES
Self-made stems for flowers, medium wide lines.

REMARKS
Lazy way: work chains first, then come back with "spines" as a second journey!

H.19 STEP STITCH

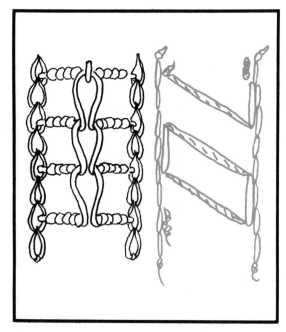

RHYTHM
Part 1: up / loop—down—up /
Part 2: up / down / up
Part 3: up / slide, slide, slide, slide, etc.

COMPOSITION
Chain stitch and straight stitches, with whipping.

USES
Wide decorative borders.

REMARKS
Place foundations in darker shades and whip in lighter shade or contrasting color for maximum effect.

D.O.W. ↓

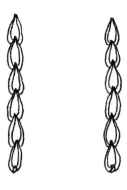

Step 1. Work two parallel rows of chain stitch, making sure chains are even and worked directly opposite on the two rows.

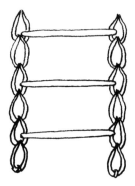

Step 2. Work a straight stitch in the *first* two chains, skip second pair, work third pair, etc.

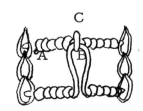

Step 3. Bring thread up at A; just below first straight stitch. Whip by sliding needle under straight stitch from top to bottom. When halfway across, make a short straight stitch (B-C) and continue whipping, but slide needle from bottom to top. Whip all straight stitches top to bottom on left, bottom to top on right. At center of second row, slide needle under straight stitch (B-C) from left to right to form the large loop. This loop is slid under the previous loop in subsequent rows.

D.O.W. ↓

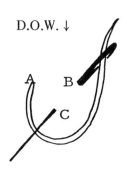

Step 1.   Bring thread up at A; pull through. Make a loop down and around to the right. Insert needle at B, bring up at C, and, with loop beneath needle, pull through.

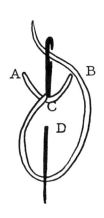

Step 2.   Make a loop down and around to the right. Insert needle again at C, to the right of the thread through C. Bring needle up at D and, with loop beneath needle, pull through. Do not pull loops tightly.

Step 3.   Insert needle again at D but outside of loop formed with Step 2.

Note

Changing proportions and tension of loops can make interesting variations. Stitches may be stacked to form a border stitch.

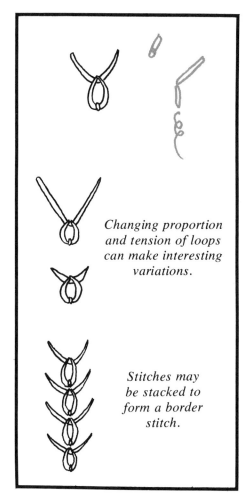

Changing proportion and tension of loops can make interesting variations.

Stitches may be stacked to form a border stitch.

RHYTHM
Up / loop down and around—down—up inside loop / loop down and around—down same hole—up inside second loop / tack.

COMPOSITION
Fly and detached chain.

USES
Isolated stitches, topsy-turvy for filling, arranged along a feather-stitch "stem" for flowers.

REMARKS
Longer "ears" make rabbits. Great when using two different shades in needle at the same time.

H.21 WAVE STITCH FILLING
Huck Weaving Stitch

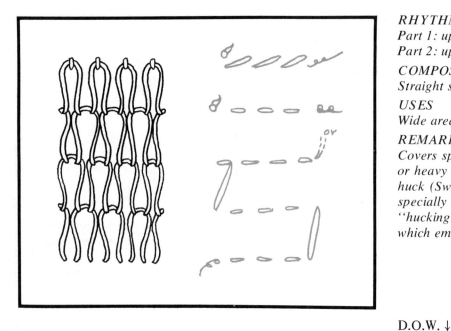

RHYTHM
Part 1: up / down / up /
Part 2: up / slide / down—up /
COMPOSITION
Straight stitch with reverse chain variation.
USES
Wide areas, geometric shapes.
REMARKS
Covers sparsely and quickly; effective with light or heavy yarns. This is the basic stitch used in huck (Swedish) weaving. It is usually done on specially woven material called "huck" or "hucking," which has raised threads through which embroidery threads are passed.

Step 1. Lay foundation of straight stitches, small and evenly spaced. Start and right end of line.

D.O.W. ↓

Step 2. Bring thread up at A; pull through. Slide needle under straight stitch (1) from left to right (do not pierce fabric); pull through loosely. Insert needle at B, bring up at C; pull through. Slide needle under straight stitch (2). Continue, alternating these two procedures until each straight stitch is filled.

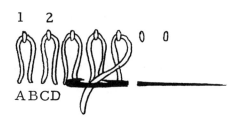

Step 3. Working from right to left, bring thread up at AA; pull through. Slide needle under base of last stitch; pull through. Continue, picking up small stitch at CC-BB and sliding needle under next two stitches on row above; alternating until row is finished. Next row is worked from left to right.

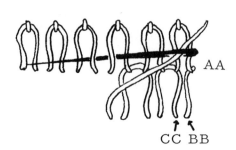

DETACHED

Step 1. Bring thread up at A; pull through. Insert needle at B, bring up again at A; pull through.

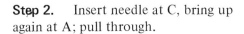

D.O.W. ↓

Step 2. Insert needle at C, bring up again at A; pull through.

Step 3. Make loop up and around to the right. Insert needle again at A, bring up at D and, loop beneath needle, pull through.

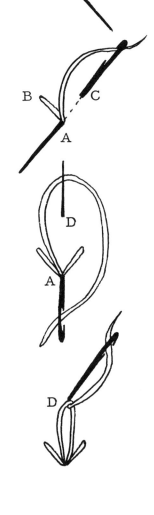

Step 4. Insert needle again at D, but *outside* of loop, and pull through.

ATTACHED

Work Steps 1 and 2 but bring up needle at D (below A-B and A-C).

Step 3a. Slide needle under straight stitches from right to left (do not pierce fabric); pull through.

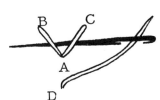

Step 4a. Insert needle again at D, up at E and pull through. Continue.

Note

Reverse chain is worked (after first stitch) by sliding needle under straight stitches but *over* previous chain stitch.

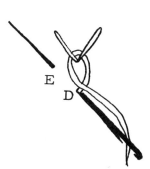

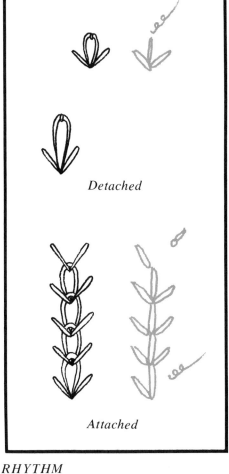

Detached

Attached

RHYTHM
Part 1: up / down / up / down /
Part 2: up—loop up and around—down same hole—up inside loop / tack

COMPOSITION
Detached: *Two straight stitches and one detached chain.*
Attached: *Two straight stitches and reverse chain.*

USES
Isolated stitches, filling, arranged in pattern for flowers or attached for borders.

REMARKS
Want to cheat a little? Work just the chain part first and then set the straight stitches on either side. Who will know?

183

H.23 WHIPPED ARROWHEAD STITCH
Raised Chevron Stitch

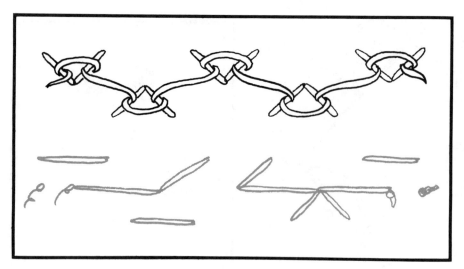

RHYTHM
Part 1: up / down, up /
Part 2: up / slide /
COMPOSITION
Arrowhead with patterned whip-
ping (surface chevron).
USES
Wide borders.
REMARKS
Use darker shade for arrowheads
and lighter or contrasting shade for
whipping.

D.O.W. →

Step 1. Lay foundation stitches, following the ABC's. (Up at A, down at B, up at C, down again at A, on to D, up, etc.)

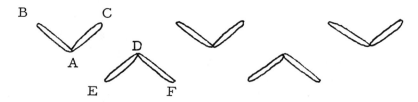

Step 2. With contrasting thread, bring needle up at AA. Slide needle under A-B from right to left; do not pierce fabric. Pull through. Holding thread above needle, slide needle under A-C from the right; pull through loosely.

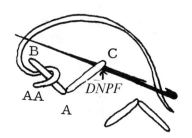

Step 3. Slide needle under E-D; pull through. Holding thread below line, slide needle under D-F and pull through loosely.

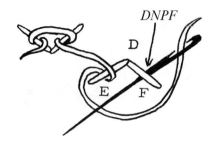

Note

The rhythm of the lacing is the same as chevron stitch.

D.O.W. ↰

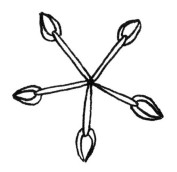

Step 1. Set in a "wheel" of long tack daisy stitches. (See daisy variations, C.2.)

Step 2. Bring thread (of contrasting color) up at A, between Stitches 1 and 2; pull through. Slide needle under long tack of stitch and stitch 2 and pull through loosely. Do not pierce fabric.

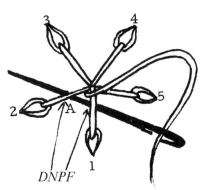

DNPF

Step 3. Continue, sliding under stitch just slid under and the next one, all in one motion. Be sure to keep thread toward the middle and out of the way. Work four or five rounds for best effect. To finish, bring thread through to the back and knot off.

DNPF

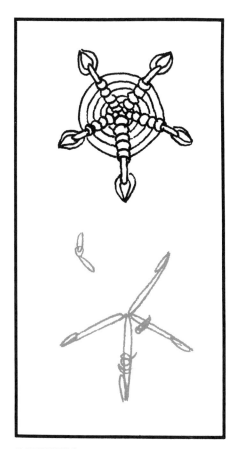

RHYTHM
Part 1: up / loop down and around to right—down same hole—up over loop /
Part 2: up / around and under one plus one

COMPOSITION
Long-tack daisy and whipping.

USES
Complete flowers, flower centers, snow flakes.

REMARKS
Try substituting Italian knots (long-tack knots) for daisy to make a more delicate design. Remember to whip loosely! The more times around, the higher the middle will stand up.

Color contrasts are important; usually looks better if dark shade is used for base and lighter shade for whipping. Don't go too close to the chain part; fill in just around center.

COUCHED OR LAID STITCHES

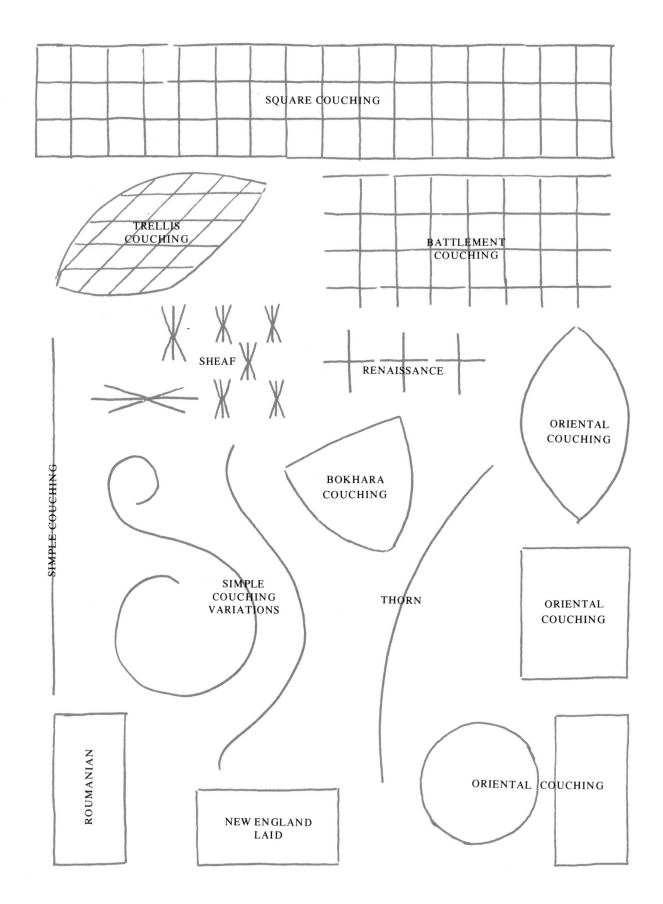

SQUARE COUCHING

TRELLIS COUCHING

BATTLEMENT COUCHING

SHEAF

RENAISSANCE

ORIENTAL COUCHING

SIMPLE COUCHING

BOKHARA COUCHING

SIMPLE COUCHING VARIATIONS

THORN

ORIENTAL COUCHING

ROUMANIAN

NEW ENGLAND LAID

ORIENTAL COUCHING

family I Couched or Laid Stitches

Basic rhythm: (Part one) up / down /
(Part two) up / down / over laid thread

Progression of difficulty

Isolated 1. SHEAF, FILLING AND VARIATIONS
2. RENAISSANCE

Line 3. SIMPLE COUCHING (Couching, Laid Work)
4. SIMPLE COUCHING VARIATIONS
5. THORN

Stacked 6. ROUMANIAN
7. NEW ENGLAND LAID (Deerfield)
8. BOKHARA COUCHING
9. ORIENTAL COUCHING

Combined 10. SQUARE COUCHING
11. TRELLIS COUCHING (Jacobean Couching)
12. BATTLEMENT COUCHING

I.1 SHEAF STITCH, FILLING AND VARIATIONS

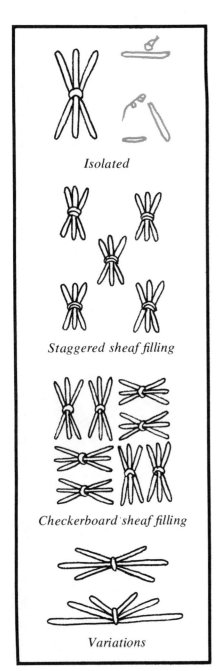

Isolated

Staggered sheaf filling

Checkerboard sheaf filling

Variations

RHYTHM
Up / down—up /

USES
Isolated stitches, border stitches, filling stitches.

REMARKS
A lovely zig-zag line may be worked by stacking this stitch, one on top of the other, and working the second stitch into the same holes as the bottom of the first. Save some time by working three parallel rows of Holbein stitch and then gathering all the centers on the last journey.

Step 1.   Bring thread up at A; pull through. Insert needle at B, up at C; pull through.

Step 2.   Insert needle at D, bring up at E; pull through.

Step 3.   Insert needle at F; pull through. (Three parallel straight stitches are formed.) Bring needle up at G (on a line with A-B) pushing stitch A-B over slightly so G is hidden by A-B. Pull through.

Step 4.   Slide needle under stitch E-F (from right to left), do not pierce fabric; pull through.

Step 5.   Slide needle under D-C from right to left; do not pierce fabric. Pull through loosely, leaving loop.

Step 6.   Insert needle again at G, to the right of stitch A-B. Pull loop up tightly.

Note

Threads may be wrapped a second time (Steps 4 and 5) before insertion at G (Step 6). See staggered sheaf filling.

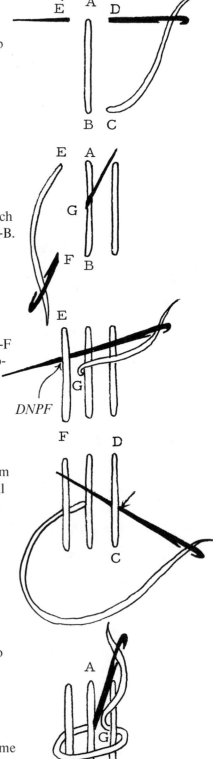

D.O.W. Any

DNPF

D.O.W. Any

Step 1.   Bring thread up at A; pull through. Holding thread to the left, insert needle at B, bring up at C; pull through.

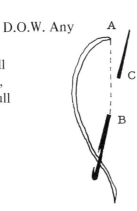

Step 2.   Insert needle at D, bring up again at A; pull through.

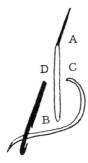

Step 3.   Holding thread to the left, insert needle again at B, bring up again at D; pull through A very loosely.

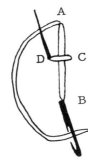

Step 4.   Insert needle at E, bring up again at A; pull through.

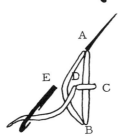

Step 5.   Holding thread to the right, insert needle again at B, bring up again at C; pull through loosely.

Step 6.   Insert at F; pull through.

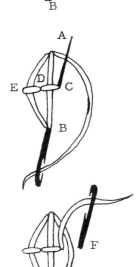

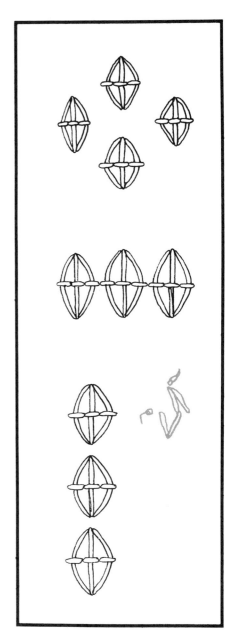

RHYTHM
Up / down—up / down—up / loop left—down—up / down—up / loop right—down—up / down /

USES
Isolated stitches, border stitches, filling stitches.

REMARKS
Many possibilities in spacing and arrangement make this a versatile stitch.

I.3 SIMPLE COUCHING
Laid Work

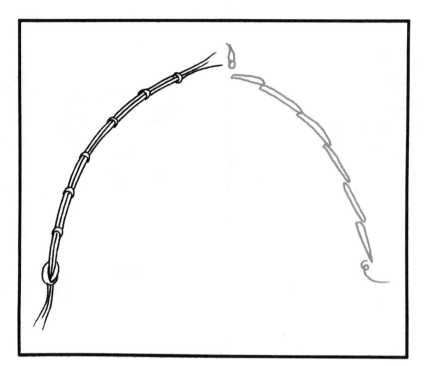

RHYTHM
Part 1: up / leave thread loose
Part 2: up / down /
USES
When thread to be used is too thick to go through fabric easily, or when gold thread is used (as in ecclesiastic embroidery) and all of it appears on the surface.
REMARKS
The ends of the heavy thread may be left on the surface of the fabric and knotted or couched in an interesting pattern. If thread is too heavy to go through a needle's eye, pull to back with a small crochet hook.

D.O.W. ↙

Step 1.   Lay heavy thread (or bundle of threads) along line to be covered. With contrasting single thread, bring thread up at A, over bundle and back down at A, making a small loop to hold bundle in place.

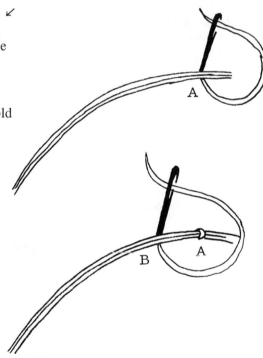

Step 2.   Bring thread up at B, over bundle and back down at B; pull through.

Note

Heavy thread may be clipped short and left on surface at start and finish, it may be knotted and tacked down, or it may be brought to the back (with a large needle or crochet hook) and knotted.

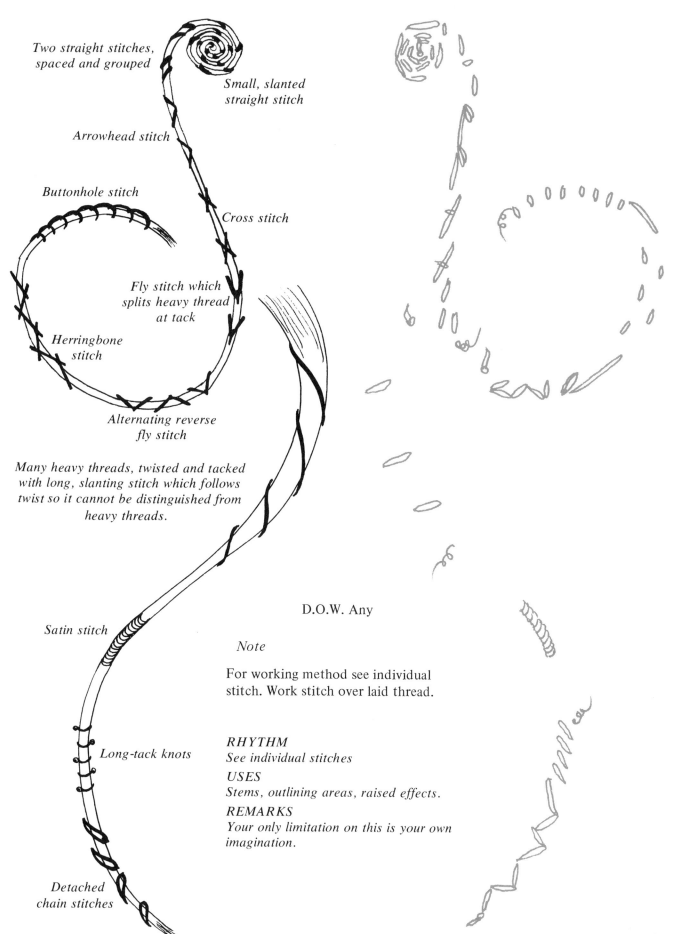

Two straight stitches,
spaced and grouped

Small, slanted
straight stitch

Arrowhead stitch

Buttonhole stitch

Cross stitch

Fly stitch which
splits heavy thread
at tack

Herringbone
stitch

Alternating reverse
fly stitch

Many heavy threads, twisted and tacked
with long, slanting stitch which follows
twist so it cannot be distinguished from
heavy threads.

Satin stitch

D.O.W. Any

Note

For working method see individual
stitch. Work stitch over laid thread.

Long-tack knots

RHYTHM
See individual stitches
USES
Stems, outlining areas, raised effects.
REMARKS
Your only limitation on this is your own
imagination.

Detached
chain stitches

I.5 THORN STITCH

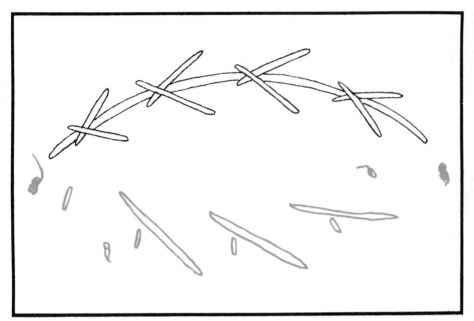

D.O.W. →

RHYTHM
Part 1: up / down / end off
Part 2: up / down—up / etc.

USES
Stems, wide lines.

REMARKS
Although traditionally worked on a curve, this stitch can be worked on a straight line as a border stitch. Take care to keep it very even.

Step 1. With heavy thread, bring up at A, cover line, insert at B; pull through and knot off.

Step 2. With light contrasting thread, bring up at C; pull through. Insert needle at D, bring up at E; pull through.

Step 3. Insert needle at F (may be pulled through at this point to complete first stitch). Continue with G; pull through, etc.

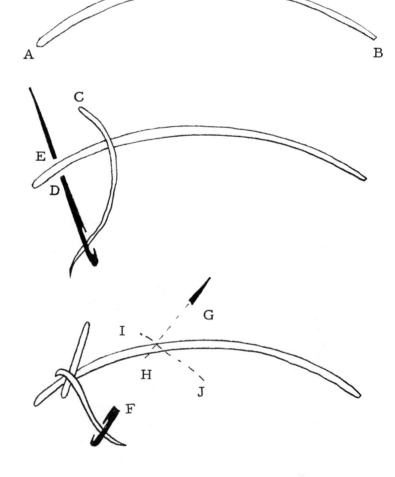

D.O.W. ←

Step 1. Bring thread up at A; pull through. Holding thread to the left, insert needle at B; bring up at C; pull through.

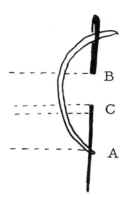

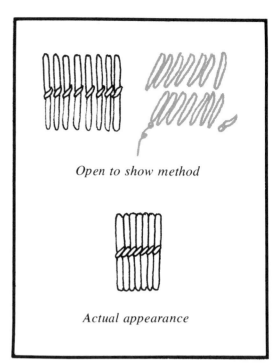

Open to show method

Actual appearance

Step 2. Holding thread to the right, insert needle at D (thus completing small slanting stitch over B-A), bring up at E; pull through.

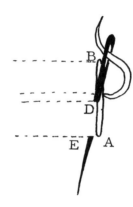

RHYTHM
Up / down—up / down—up /

USES
Solid filling stitches, leaf shapes with "vein" running down center.

REMARKS
When a satin-like filling is needed, but the space to be filled would make individual stitches too long, substitute this stitch.

Step 3. Continue, setting second stitch close to first so that no fabric shows through between.

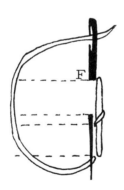

I.7 NEW ENGLAND LAID STITCH
Deerfield Stitch

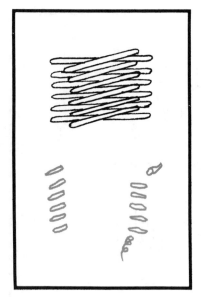

RHYTHM
Up / down—up /

USES
Wide, solidly filled lines and areas.

REMARKS
Very much like Roumanian stitch except tacking stitch is longer.

D.O.W. ↓

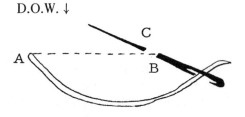

Step 1. Bring thread up at A; pull through. Insert needle at B, bring up at C; pull through.

Step 2. Insert needle at D (thus completing a long slanting stitch across A-B), bring up at E and pull through.

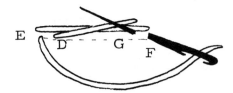

Step 3. Insert needle at F, bring up at G, pull through and continue with Step 2. Stitches should be worked very close together.

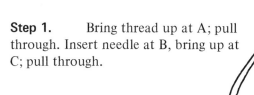

Step 1.   Bring thread up at A; pull through. Insert needle at B, bring up at C; pull through.

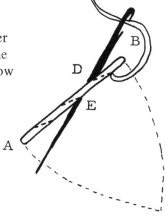

Step 2.   Insert needle at D (thus completing a small slanting stitch over A-B), bring up at E; pull through. The small dotted lines over stitch A-B show where next stitches will be placed.

Note

When long stitch is tacked in several places forming a pattern, the stitch is called *Bokhara* to differentiate it from Roumanian stitch.

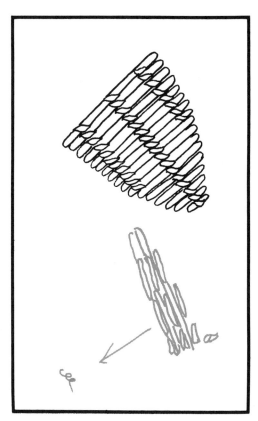

RHYTHM
Up / down—up / tack—tack—tack

USES
Filling.

REMARKS
Covers large areas very well and may be tacked as frequently as desired. A stitch which will wear well (on a pillow, for example) and stay in place despite much handling.

I.9 ORIENTAL COUCHING

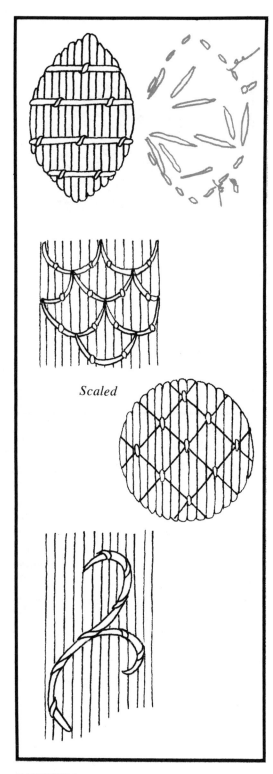

Scaled

RHYTHM
Up / down / up /

USES
Filling wide areas.

REMARKS
Because the satin stitch will be tacked, a much longer stitch than usual may be used.

D.O.W. Any

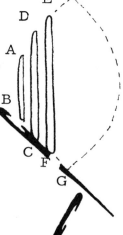

Step 1. Lay stitches so that space (width of one thread) remains between. Needle shows direction of stitches.

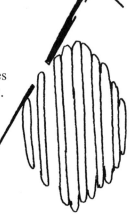

Step 2. Second journey. Lay stitches between those worked in first journey. (This method saves thread, although regular satin stitch may be used.)

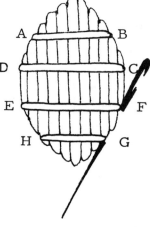

Step 3. With contrasting thread lay a few spaced stitches across the satin stitches.

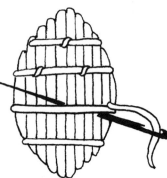

Step 4. With a third contrasting thread, tack down stitches laid in Step 3 with tiny slanting stitches to form a regular pattern.

Note

When working the scaled pattern, place overlay stitches loosely so that they may be pulled down to make the curve as subsequent rows are set.

RHYTHM
Up / down / up / etc.

USES
Covering large areas, filling, Jacobean flowers and leaves.

REMARKS
Numerous combinations will work— try them. Don't waste yarn on back. When starting next parallel row, come up at the spot nearest one where you went down before.

To work freehand, try to follow threads in fabric. Lay yarn along, hold in place, mark the spot where the other end will go down with the point of the needle, and then pull through.
Tip: lay longest threads first.

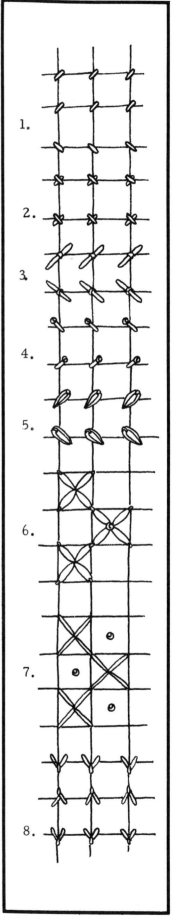

1.

2.

3.

4.

5.

6.

7.

8.

D.O.W. Any

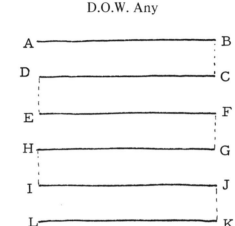

Step 1. Lay straight stitches in regular parallel lines, following threads of fabric. (Dotted line shows thread under fabric)

Step 2. Lay straight lines perpendicularly across so that perfect squares are formed.

Step 3. Simple tack: bring contrasting thread up at *a*. Pull through, insert at *b*, up at *c*, pull through. Greater accuracy is maintained using stab method.

Tacking variations

1. Short straight stitch
2. Cross stitch
3. Long and short cross stitch
4. Long tack knots
5. Detached chain
6. Four chains worked in alternate squares (French knot added in one)
7. Long straight stitches worked in alternate squares (French knots in others)
8. Fly stitch

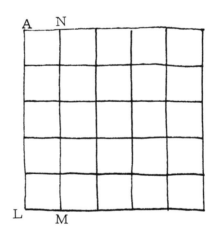

199

I.11 TRELLIS COUCHING
Jacobean Couching

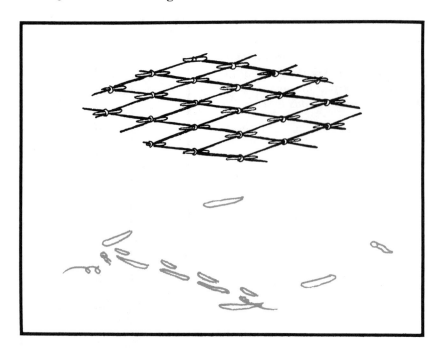

RHYTHM
Up / down / up / etc.

USES
Filling large areas, Jacobean leaves and flowers.

REMARKS
Be sure (if working freehand) that you have a true diamond shape, not just a square turned up on a corner.

Traditionally, this form is always tacked with the long tack running on the length of the diamond and the short tack crossing on the breadth.

Step 1. Bring thread up at A; pull through. Lay thread at a 45° angle to determine first stitch. (Dotted lines show straight and cross threads of fabric.)

D.O.W. Any

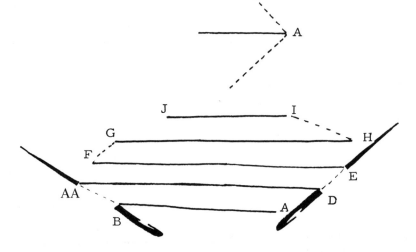

Step 2. Lay parallel straight stitches (Following ABC's) until area is covered. (Dotted lines show thread on back of fabric.)

Step 3. Lay cross threads (on straight of fabric) starting at AA. A true diamond shape will be formed.

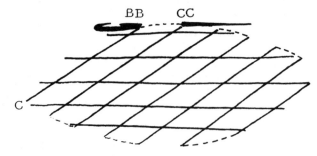

Step 4. With contrasting thread, tack at each intersection with a long straight stitch (a-b) and then, coming up at c, go over all three intersecting threads and back down at c (or very close) so that all threads are couched (tied) in place.

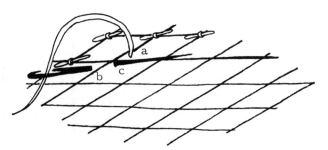

RHYTHM
Up / down / up / down

USES
Filling a large area quickly and effectively.

REMARKS
Produces a striking three-dimensional effect. Take care to lay stitches evenly and closely. The final tack stitch serves to keep the whole group in place. Best used in geometric shapes.

D.O.W. ⇄ and ↑↓

Step 1.   With darkest shade, lay first foundation stitches: up at A, down at B; pull through; up at C, pull through; down at D, pull through, etc. This is stab method and produces the most even lines.

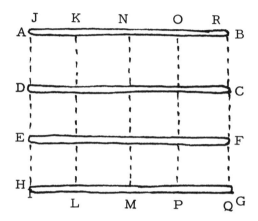

Step 2.   Come up at I, very close to H, and continue until area is covered.

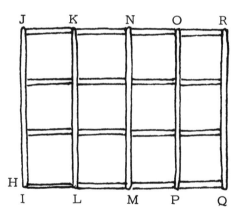

Step 3.   With second shade repeat same pattern exactly until all lines are covered. Notice: AA is *one* thread width above A, and II-JJ will be one width to the right of I-J.

Step 4.   When all shades are used (four or five usually), tack diagonally at the last intersection with contrasting color.

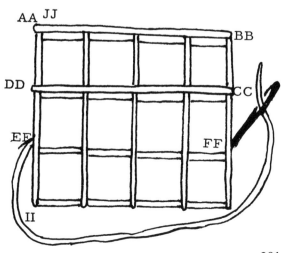

family **J**

WOVEN STITCHES

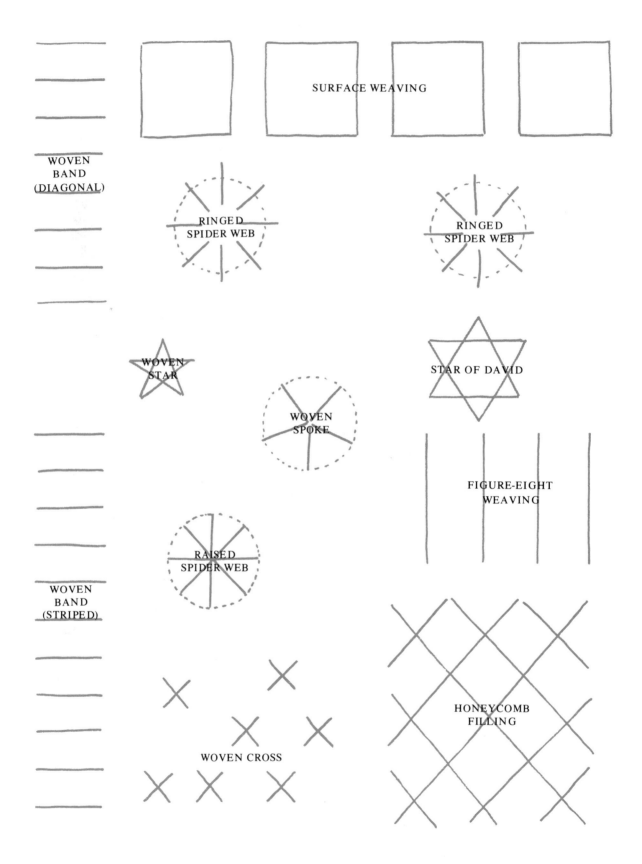

WOVEN
BAND
(DIAGONAL)

SURFACE WEAVING

RINGED
SPIDER WEB

RINGED
SPIDER WEB

WOVEN
STAR

STAR OF DAVID

WOVEN
SPOKE

WOVEN
BAND
(STRIPED)

RAISED
SPIDER WEB

FIGURE-EIGHT
WEAVING

WOVEN CROSS

HONEYCOMB
FILLING

family J   Woven Stitches

Basic rhythm: over—under, under—over

Progression of difficulty

Isolated   1. WOVEN SPOKE (Spider Web)
      2. RAISED SPIDER WEB (Ribbed or Whipped Spider Web)
      3. RINGED SPIDER WEB
      4. WOVEN CROSS
      5. WOVEN STAR (Five-pointed)
      6. STAR OF DAVID (Six-pointed)

Line   7. WOVEN BAND

Grouped   8. SURFACE AND PATTERNED WEAVING (Surface Darning)
      9. HONEYCOMB FILLING
    10. FIGURE-EIGHT WEAVING

J.1 WOVEN SPOKE STITCH
Spider Web Stitch

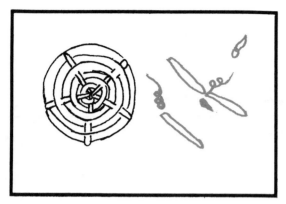

RHYTHM
Part 1: up / down / up / down / etc.
Part 2: weave over, under, over, under
USES
Large circular fillings, flower centers.
REMARKS
Weaving should be in a contrasting color for maximum effect.

Step 1. Lay foundation, an odd number of stitches radiating from center of circle.

Variation 1. Fly stitch plus two straight stitches makes five spokes.

D.O.W. Any

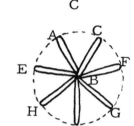

Variation 2. Up at A, down at B, up at C, down at B, etc. Makes seven spokes.

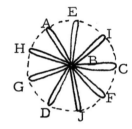

Variation 3. Same as Variation 2, makes nine spokes.

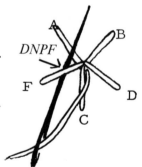

Step 2. Bring thread up close to center between C and D; pull through. Slide needle under F, over A, under B, etc., pulling through loosely after each slide under. Do not pierce fabric.

DNPF

Step 3. Continue weaving, passing under where thread passed over on previous row, and over where thread passed under. Pulling weaving thread tightly will cover spokes completely; loose weaving will expose spokes, making a pretty effect when contrasting threads are used for spokes and weaving threads. Continue until wheel is full. Insert needle at last spoke passed under, pull through to the back and knot off.

D.O.W. ↓

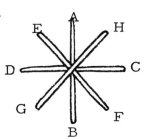

Step 1.   Lay foundation stitches. Bring thread up at A; pull through. Insert needle at B, bring up at C; pull through. Continue, down at D, up at E, down at F, up at G, down at H.

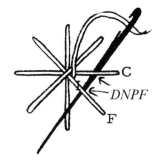

Step 2.   Bring thread up between F and C, very close to center. Slide needle under C and F; pull through. (Always pull whipping toward center.)

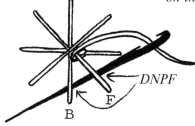

RHYTHM
Part 1: up / down / up / down
Part 2: up / slide under one / slide under one plus another /

USES
Raised circular areas, flowers, flower centers.

REMARKS
When setting in spokes (if working over a printed pattern) make them a little longer, outside the circle. The last round will cover the printed line only if extra thread is allowed on the spokes.

Step 3.   Slide needle under F and B; pull through. Continue, going back under last stitch and under next stitch, around and around, until wheel is completely filled.

Note

To raise center, hold all threads where they cross at the center with a hair pin or a short length of thread slipped underneath, and pull away from fabric while whipping. Pack threads in very closely.

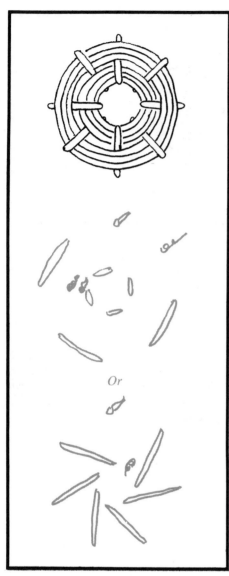

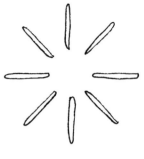

D.O.W. ↘

Step 1. Lay foundation of straight stitches in a circle, but do not bring stitches all the way in to the center.

Step 2. Based on *even* number of stitches, weave over one thread, under next, over next, etc. After a few rows, weave under two stitches, and continue weaving over one and under one.

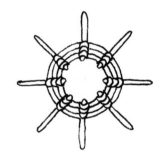

VARIATION 1. Whip by going back over stitch, then under same stitch and second stitch before pulling through.

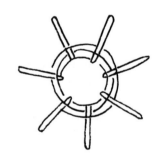

VARIATION 2. Foundation of uneven number of straight stitches will produce regular weaving (over one, under next, etc.). To finish, bring thread to back of fabric by inserting needle *under* straight stitch.

RHYTHM
Part 1: up / down /
Part 2: up / slide /
USES
Circular areas, flowers.
REMARKS
Worked in heavier yarns, the effect is bolder. Do not pull too tightly or weaving will overlap. Use darker shades for foundations, lighter for whipping.

D.O.W. Any

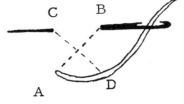

Step 1. Bring thread up at A; pull through. Insert needle at B, bring up at C; pull through.

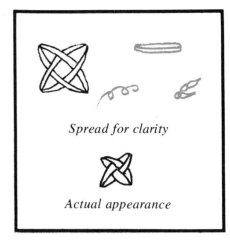

Spread for clarity

Actual appearance

Step 2. Insert needle at D, bring up again at A; pull through.

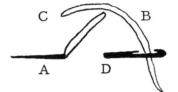

RHYTHM
Up / down—up / down. Repeat same pattern. Up / down—up / slide under base stitch only—down /

USES
Decorative borders, grouped for tiny flowers, heavy lines.

REMARKS
Makes a heavier filling than single cross stitch, but is very pretty. Most effective if second cross is a lighter shade or different color. Change color at Step 2 and do not come up again at A with first color.

Step 3. Insert needle at B, bring up at D, pull through. With needle, push first A-B up in a slight curve.

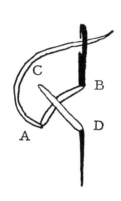

Step 4. Slide needle under first stitch in A-B and pull through. Do not pierce fabric. Insert needle at D, pull through to back and end off.

DNPF →

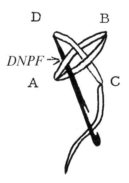

J.5 WOVEN STAR STITCH (Five-Pointed)

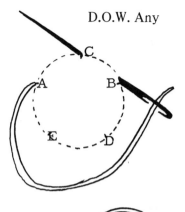

Divide a circle into five equal parts.

Step 1. Bring thread up at A; pull through. Insert needle at B, bring up at C; pull through.

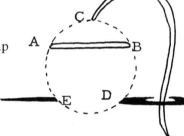

Step 2. Insert needle at D, bring up at E; pull through.

RHYTHM
Up / down—up / down—up / slide under —down / up / slide under—down / up / slide under—down /

USES
Flags, shields with American eagle, small star-shaped flowers.

REMARKS
Remember, each of five holes on circumference of circle has two threads in it and each stitch has one thread crossing over and one crossing under.

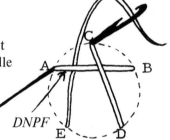

Step 3. Slide needle under stitch at A-B; do not pierce fabric. Insert needle again at C (same hole), bring up at A (same hole) and pull through.

DNPF

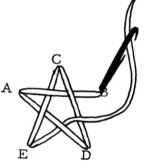

Step 4. Slide needle under stitch E-C. Insert needle at D, bring up at E; pull through.

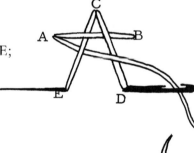

Step 5. Slide needle under stitch at A-D. Insert at B and pull through.

RHYTHM
Up / down / up / down /

USES
Star shapes, traditional Jewish embroideries.

REMARKS
Although charming worked singly, try working a smaller star inside the first and then another inside the first two. It gives a more solid effect.

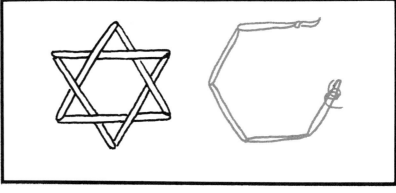

D.O.W. ↘

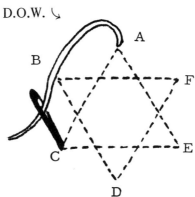

Step 1. Bring thread up at A; pull through. Insert needle at C; pull through to back. Bring needle up at B; pull through.

Step 2. Insert needle at D; pull through to back. Bring needle up at C, pull through and insert at E; pull through. Continue: up at D, down at F, up at E, down at A and up at F, pulling through between each "stab".

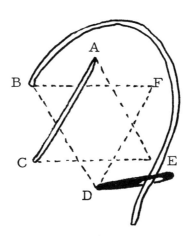

Step 3. Slide needle under A-C; do not pierce fabric. Insert at B, pull through to back and end off.

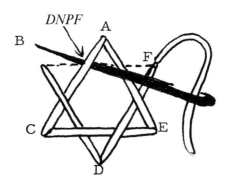

Note

All weaving is automatic except last stitch.

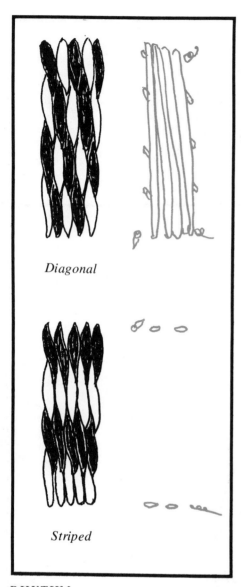

Diagonal

Striped

D.O.W. ↓

Step 1.   Lay foundation of straight stitches. Bring thread up at A; pull through. Insert at B, bring up at C, pull through, etc., until all straight stitches are laid.

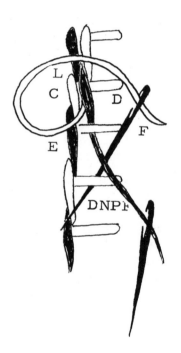

Step 2.   Thread two needles with contrasting threads. With dark thread, bring needle up just above first straight stitch (A-B) and pull through. With light thread, bring needle up at L (just above second stitch C-D) and pull through. After sliding dark thread under C-D, twist light thread over and slide needle under stitch E-F. Do not pierce fabric. Continue to end; insert needle, pull through and end off both threads. Second row (shown) starts at N with light thread so colors will alternate. Continue, weaving and twisting until band is filled.

RHYTHM
Up / down / up /

USES
Wide, raised borders.

REMARKS
The success of the weaving depends on even tension and choice of color and shade combinations.

Note

Second figure always starts with the same color to give striped effect.

D.O.W. → and ↓

Step 1. Lay foundation of satin stitch (see A.9).

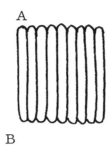

A

B

Step 2. With contrasting thread, bring needle up at *a*; pull through. Weave needle over one foundation thread, under next, over next, etc., to end. Pull through. Insert needle at *b* and pull through to back.

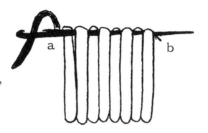

Step 3. Bring needle up at *c* (next to *b*) and pull through. Weave over thread which was crossed under in Step 2, under where thread was crossed over, etc.

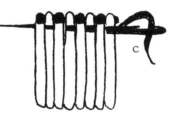

Note

Many variations may be achieved by crossing over two or three stitches in either direction. Use graph paper to plan patterns and repeats of patterns.

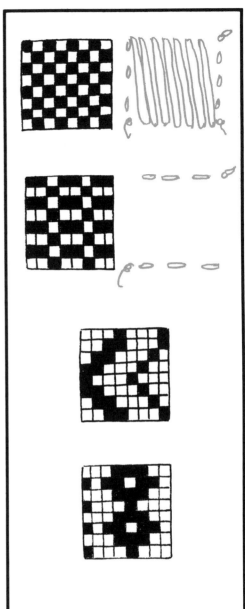

RHYTHM
Up / down / over—under—over—under, etc.

USES
Solid filling, will cover a hole.

REMARKS
Now you can cover that moth-hole or mend your socks!

J.9 HONEYCOMB FILLING

RHYTHM
Up / down /
USES
Covering large areas.
REMARKS
The closer the foundation stitches are set, the more solid will be the filling. If they are too closely set, the last weaving will be difficult and the effect lost.

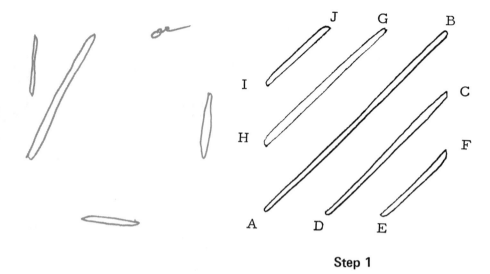

Step 1

D.O.W. Any

Step 1.   Lay foundation stitches. It is easier to place center thread first, complete one side and then the other. Bring thread up at A, pull through, down at B, up at C, pull through etc.

Step 2.   Lay second foundation stitches at right angles, over first foundation. Do not weave.

Step 3.   Bring thread up at 1; pull through. Weave over and under as shown in diagram; do not pierce fabric. Insert needle at 2, bring up at 3; pull through. Weave across to 4. Continue in this manner until area is filled.

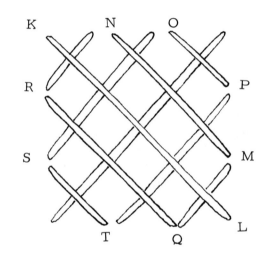

Step 2

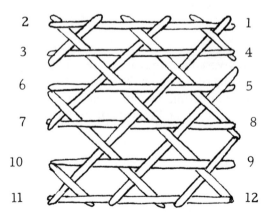

Step 3

RHYTHM
Weave under—over / turn—weave over—
under

USES
Very wide areas.

REMARKS
This may be worked over drawn threads
in coarse fabric (like burlap or monk's
cloth). Pull the weft threads (about two to
three inches) and group warp threads to
substitute for foundation stitches.

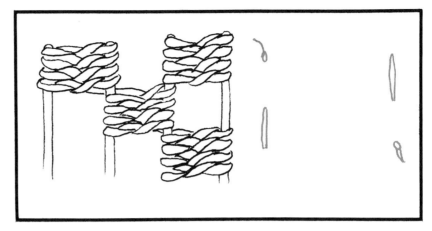

D.O.W. ↓

Step 1.   Lay foundation of straight
stitches. (Or pull threads out of fabric for one or two inches, leaving
warp threads, and weave over groups
of these threads.)

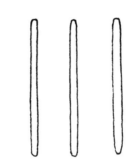

Step 2.   Bring thread up at A and
pull through. Holding thread down in
a loop, slide needle under thread as
shown on the top; pull through loosely.
Do not pierce fabric. Then slide needle
under stitch on the end over loop.
Weave in this manner four times,
pushing weaving snugly together.

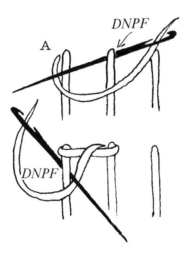

Step 3.   Slide thread under lowest
weaving in first bundle and weave
second bundle working as for Step 2.
Work will proceed on a diagonal.

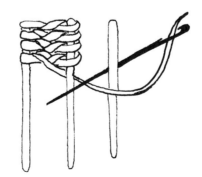

Note

Many arrangements may be formed
using varied colors in repeating "step"
patterns, diagonal or alternating
stripes, or "up and down" step
patterns.

215

Alphabetical Index of Stitches

(References are to family numbers)

Alphabetical Index of Stitches